PRESTON POTPOURRI

Volume 3

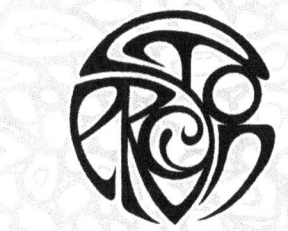

ISBN 978-0-359-00946-6

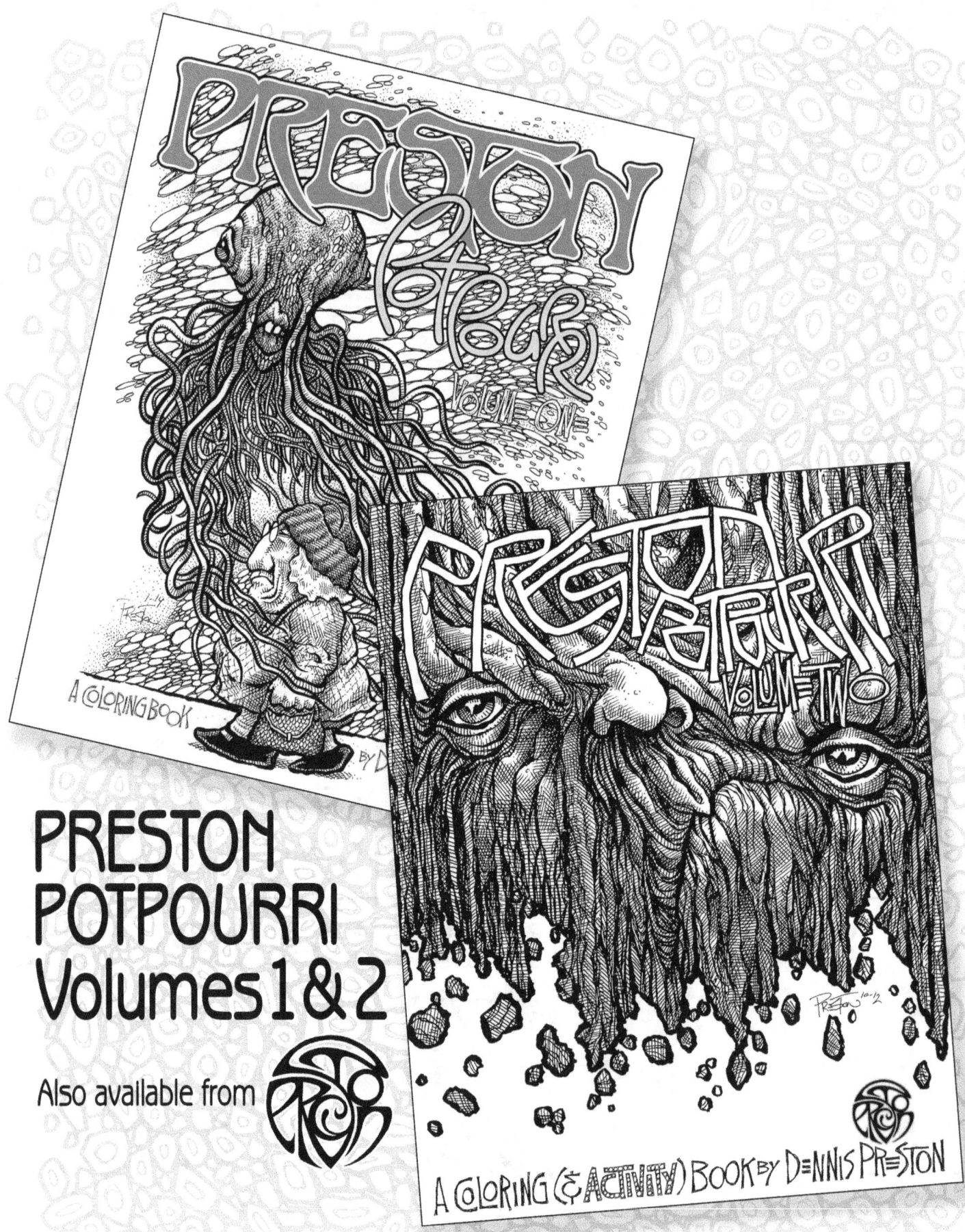

PRESTON
POTPOURRI
Volumes 1 & 2

Also available from

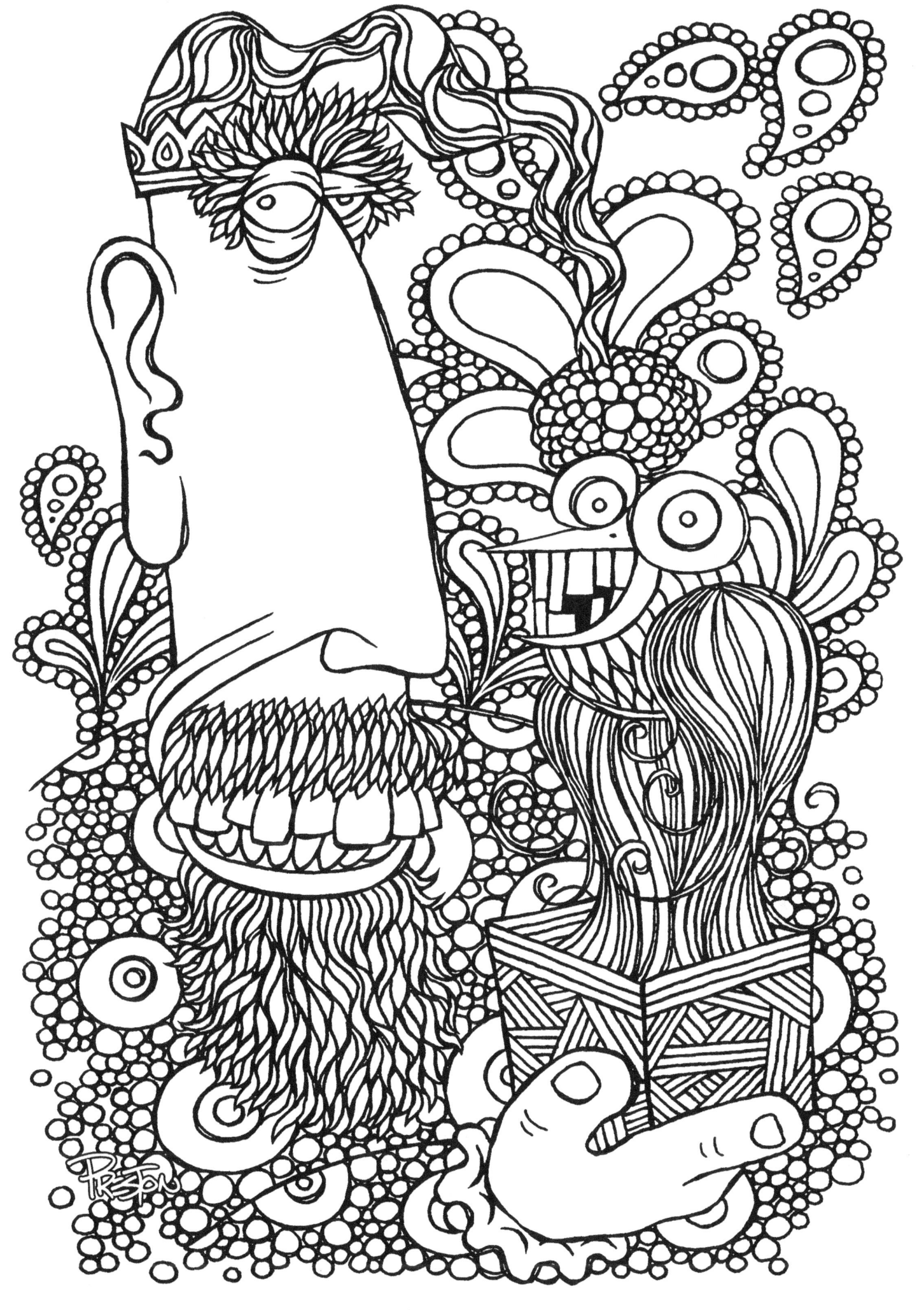

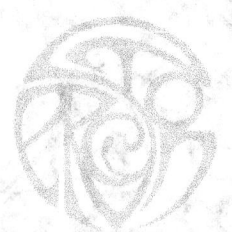

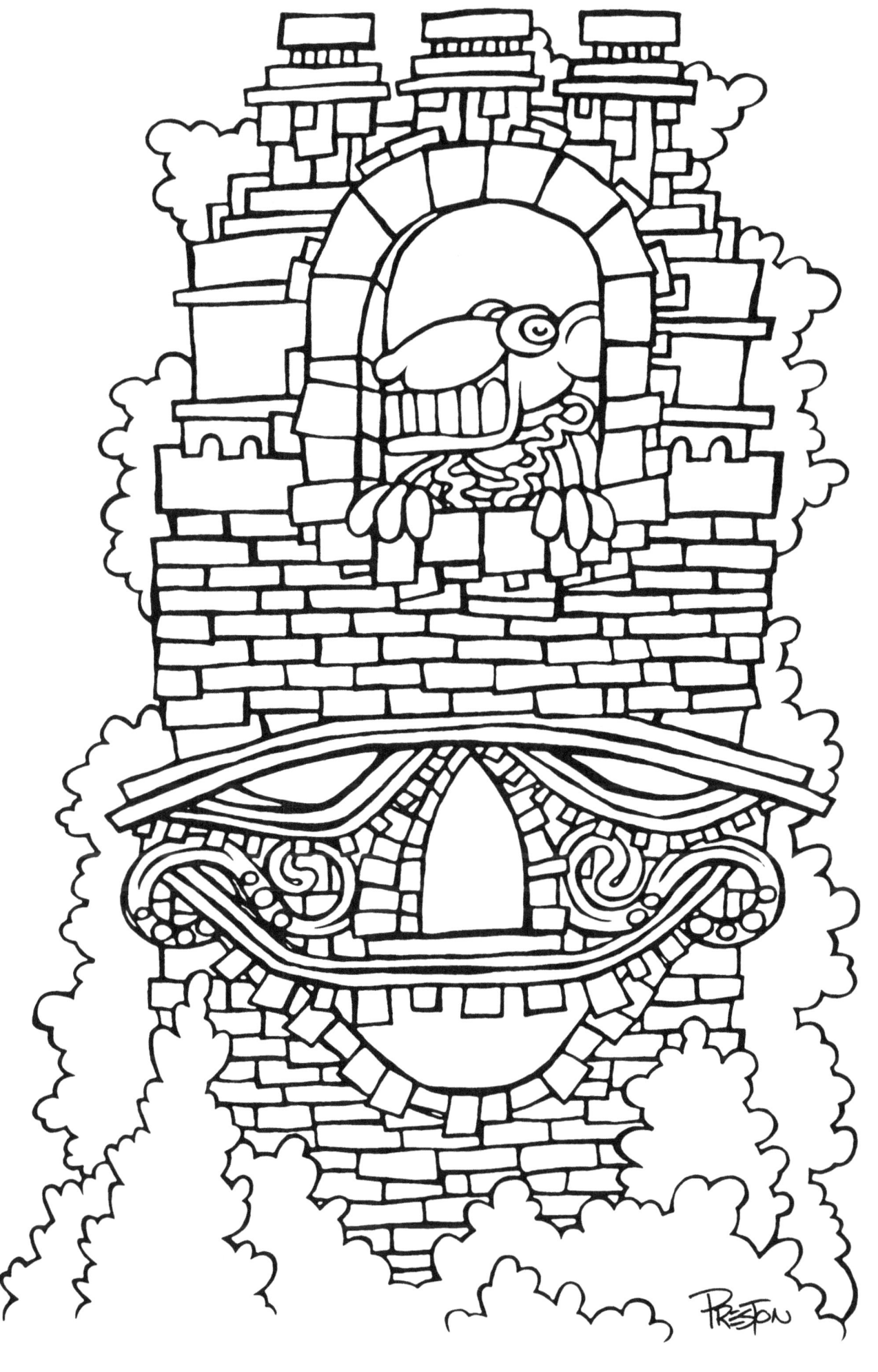

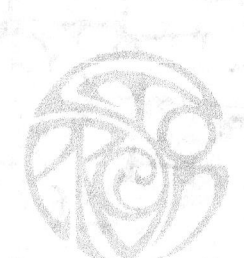

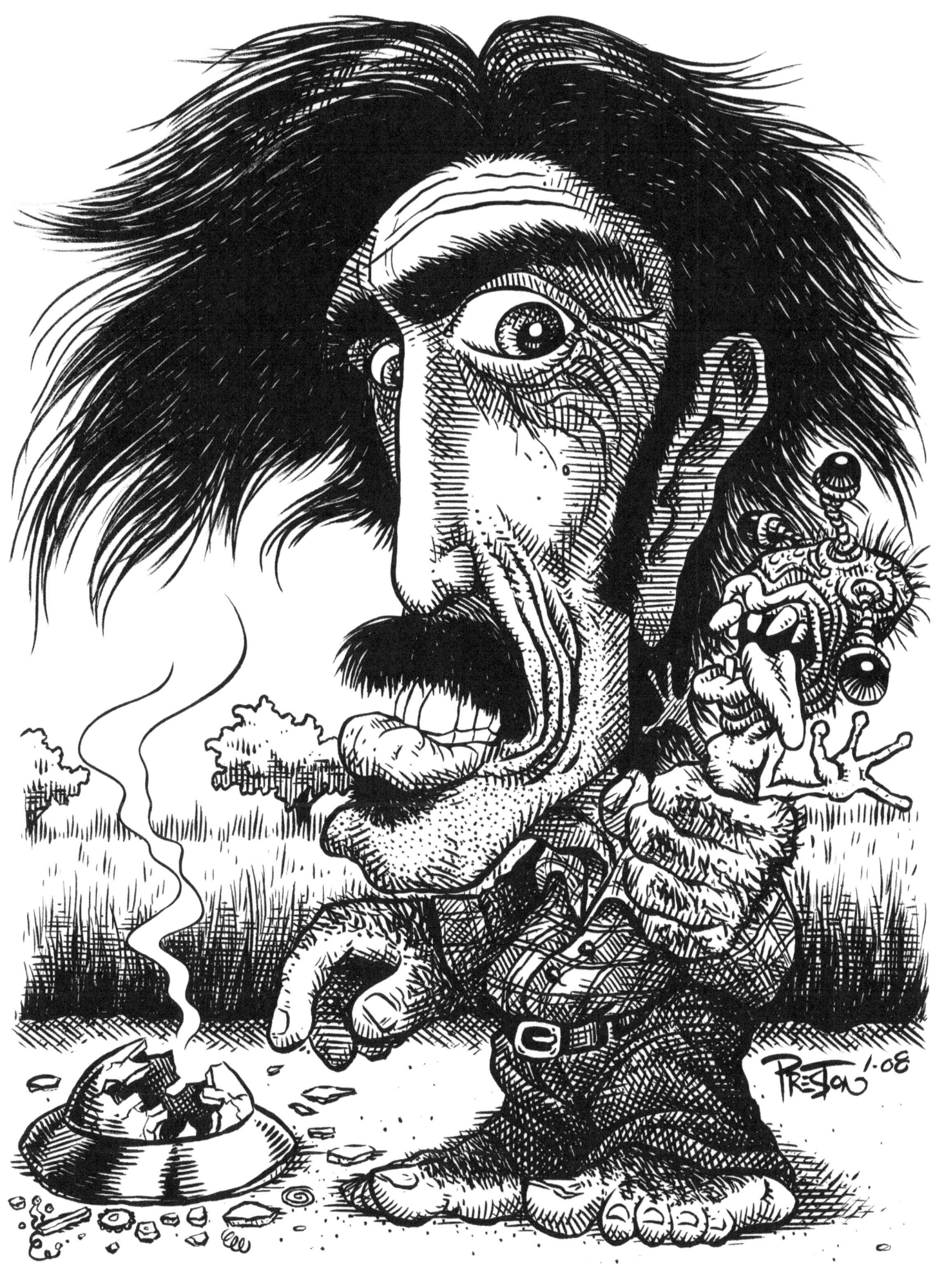

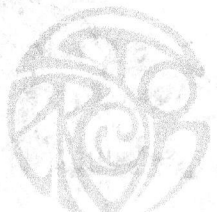

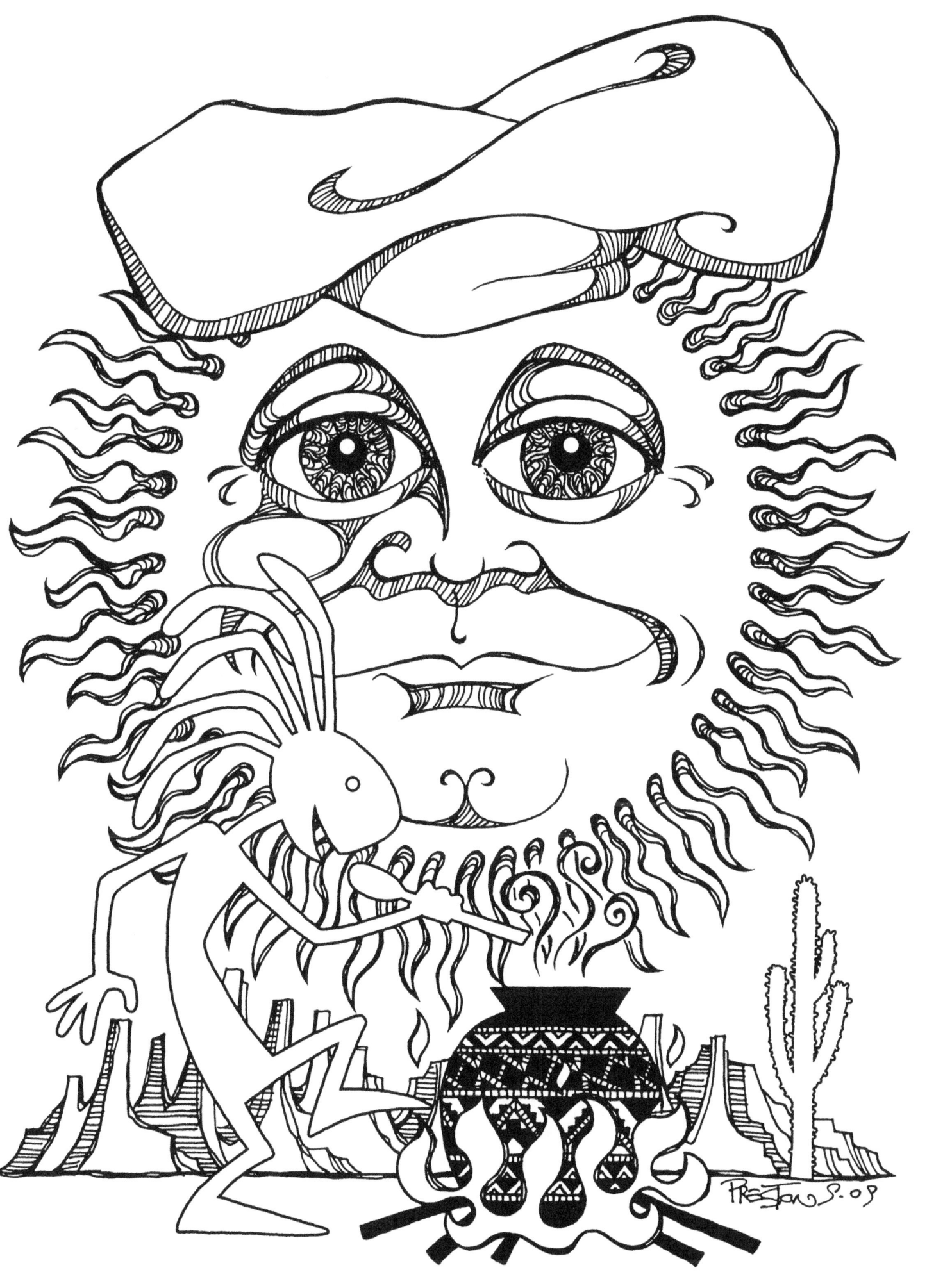

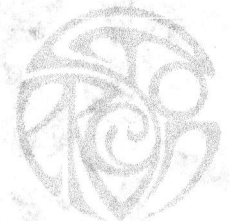

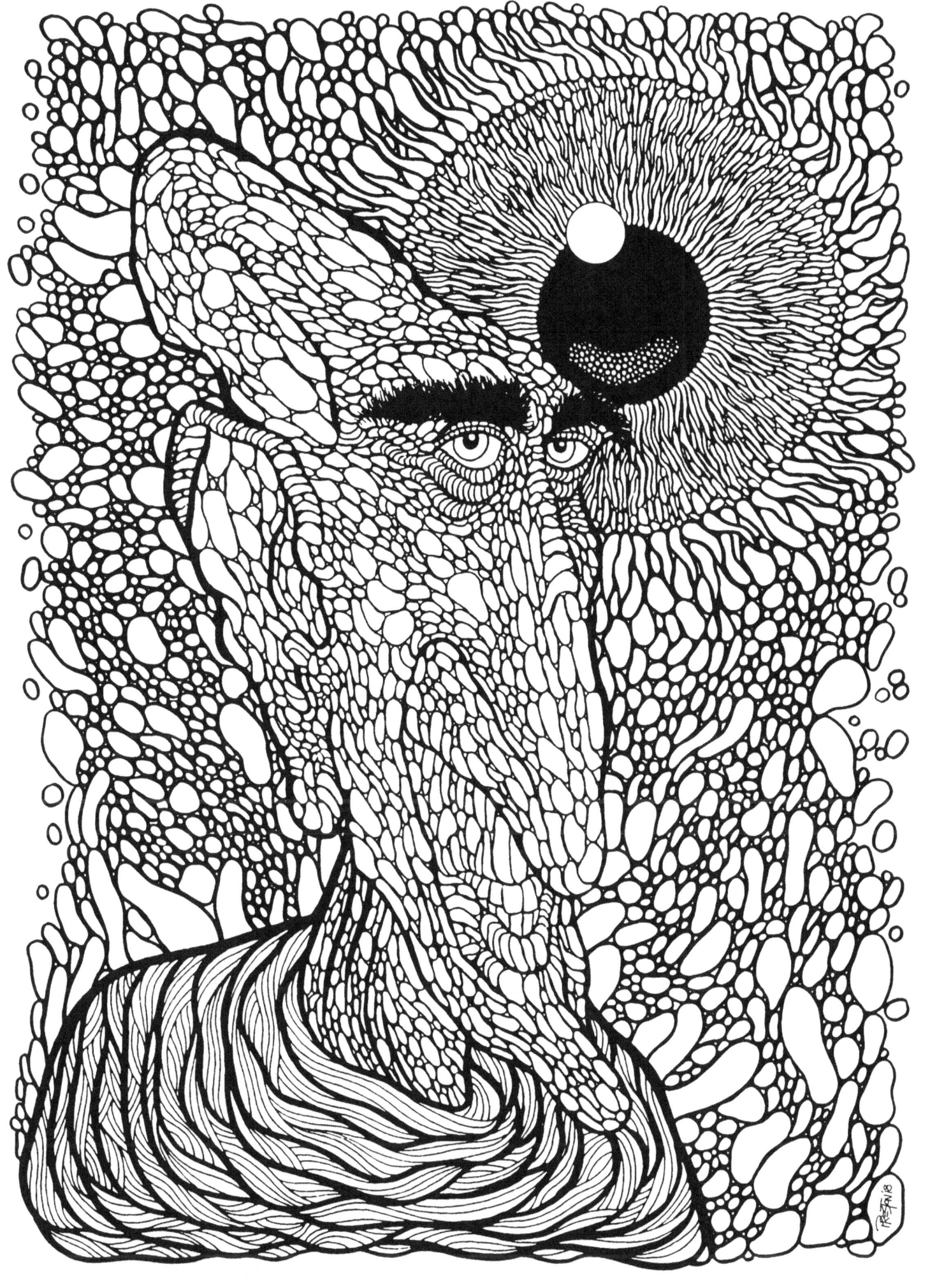

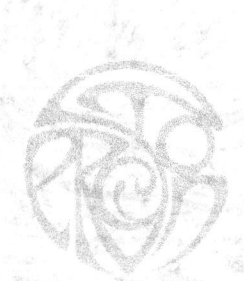

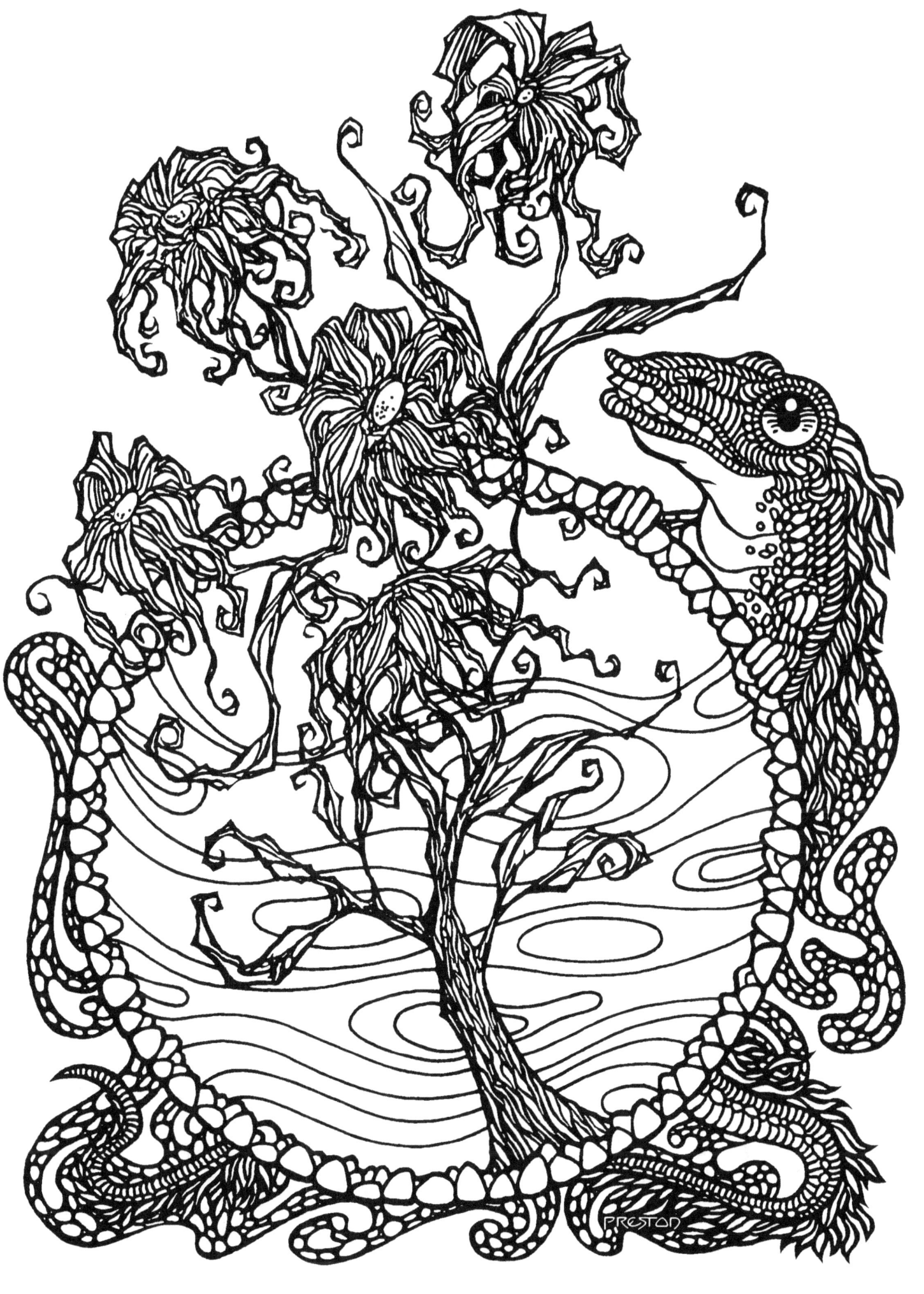

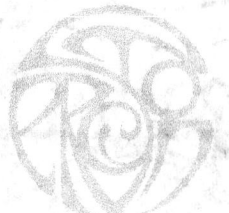

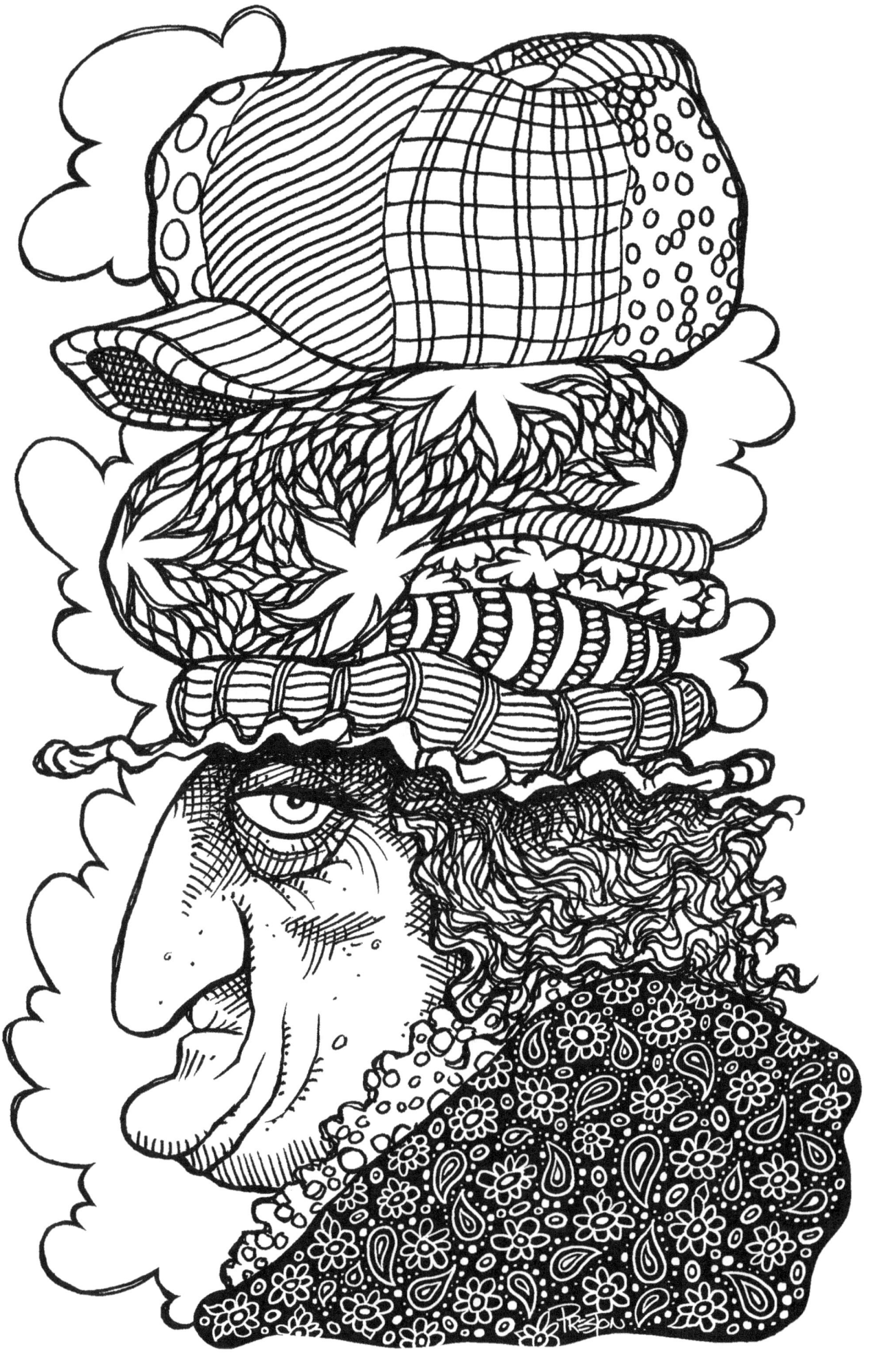

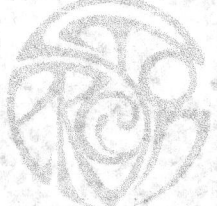

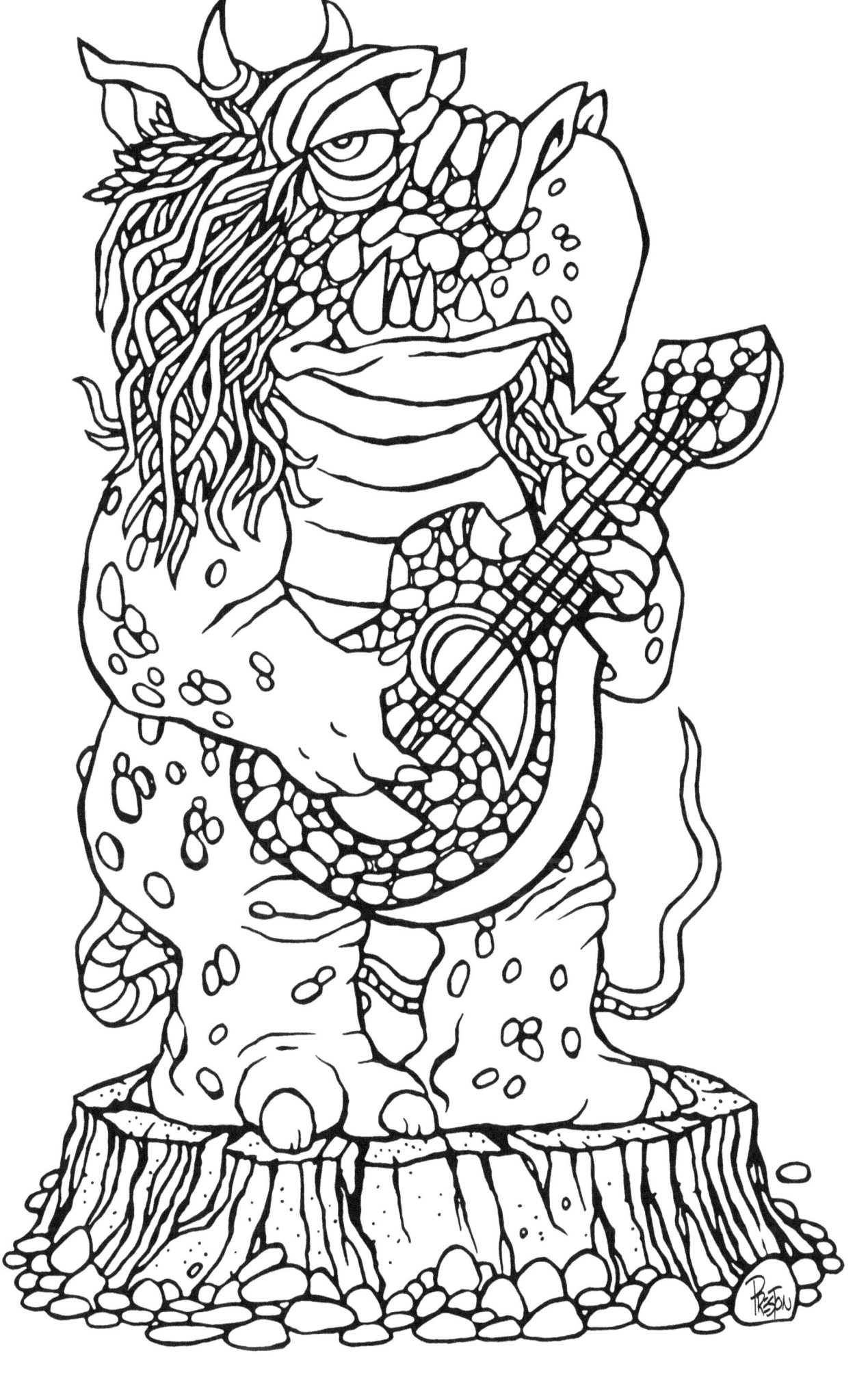

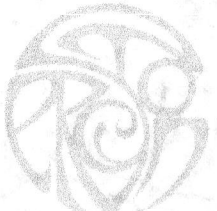

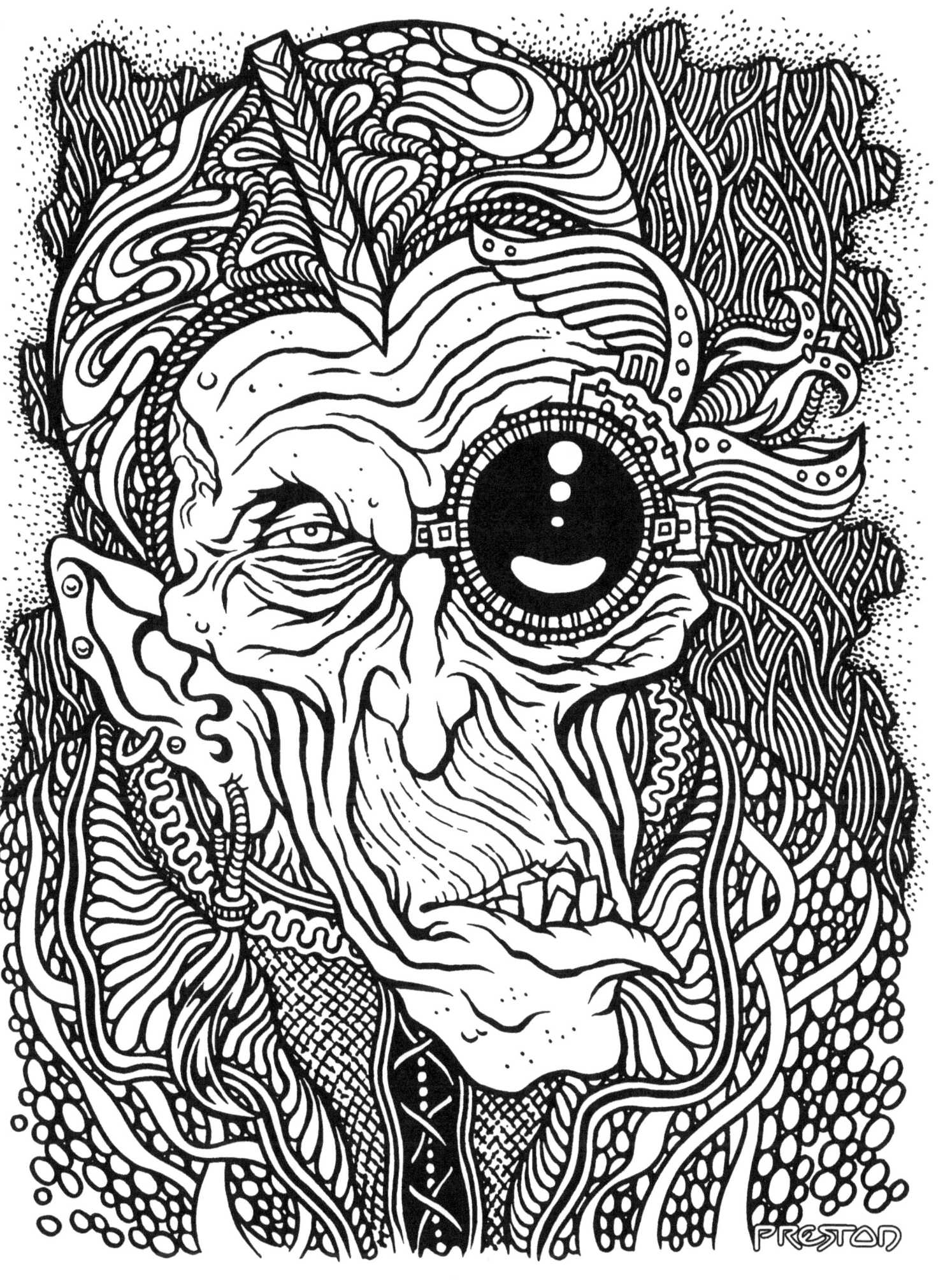

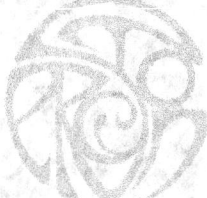

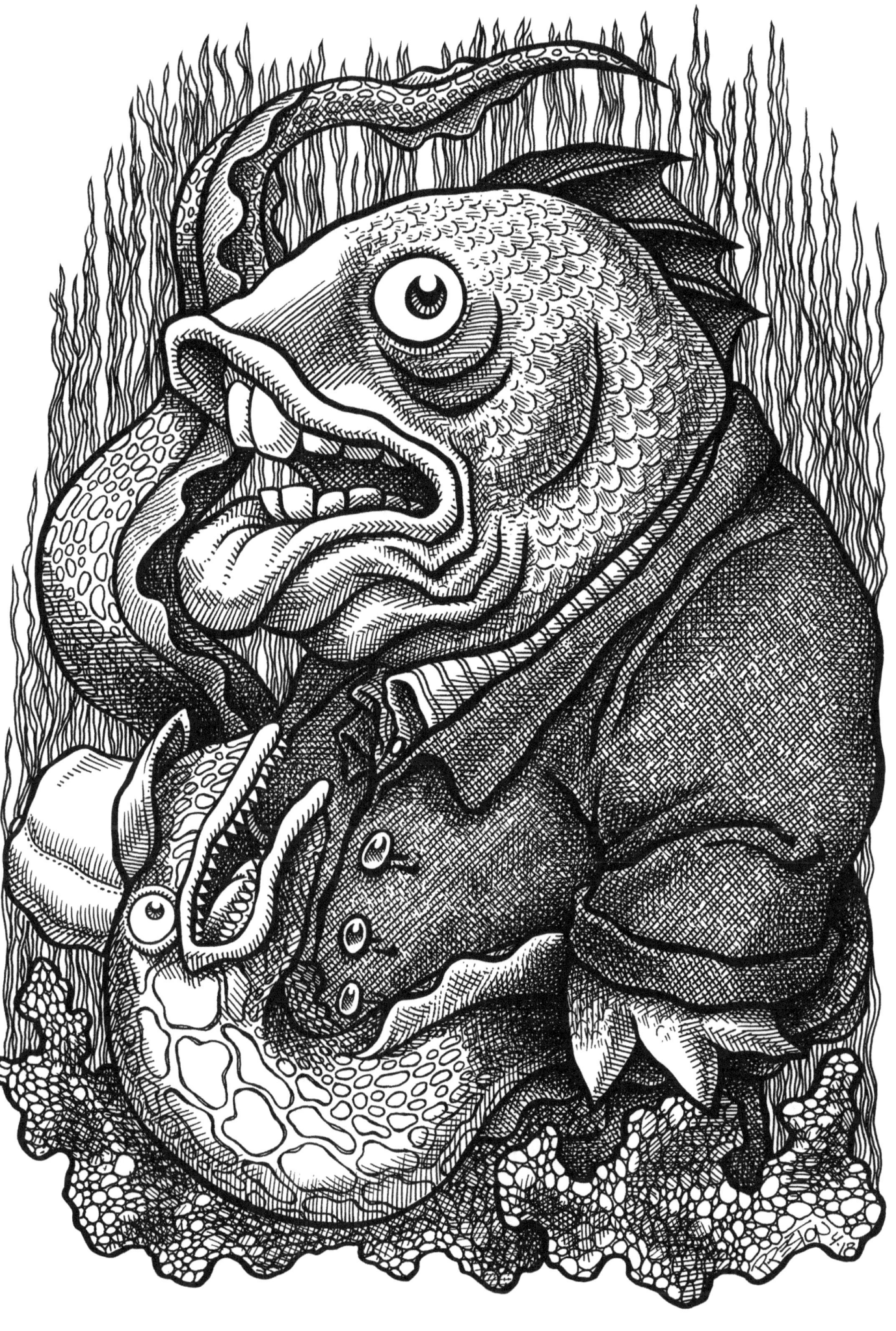

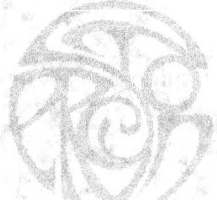

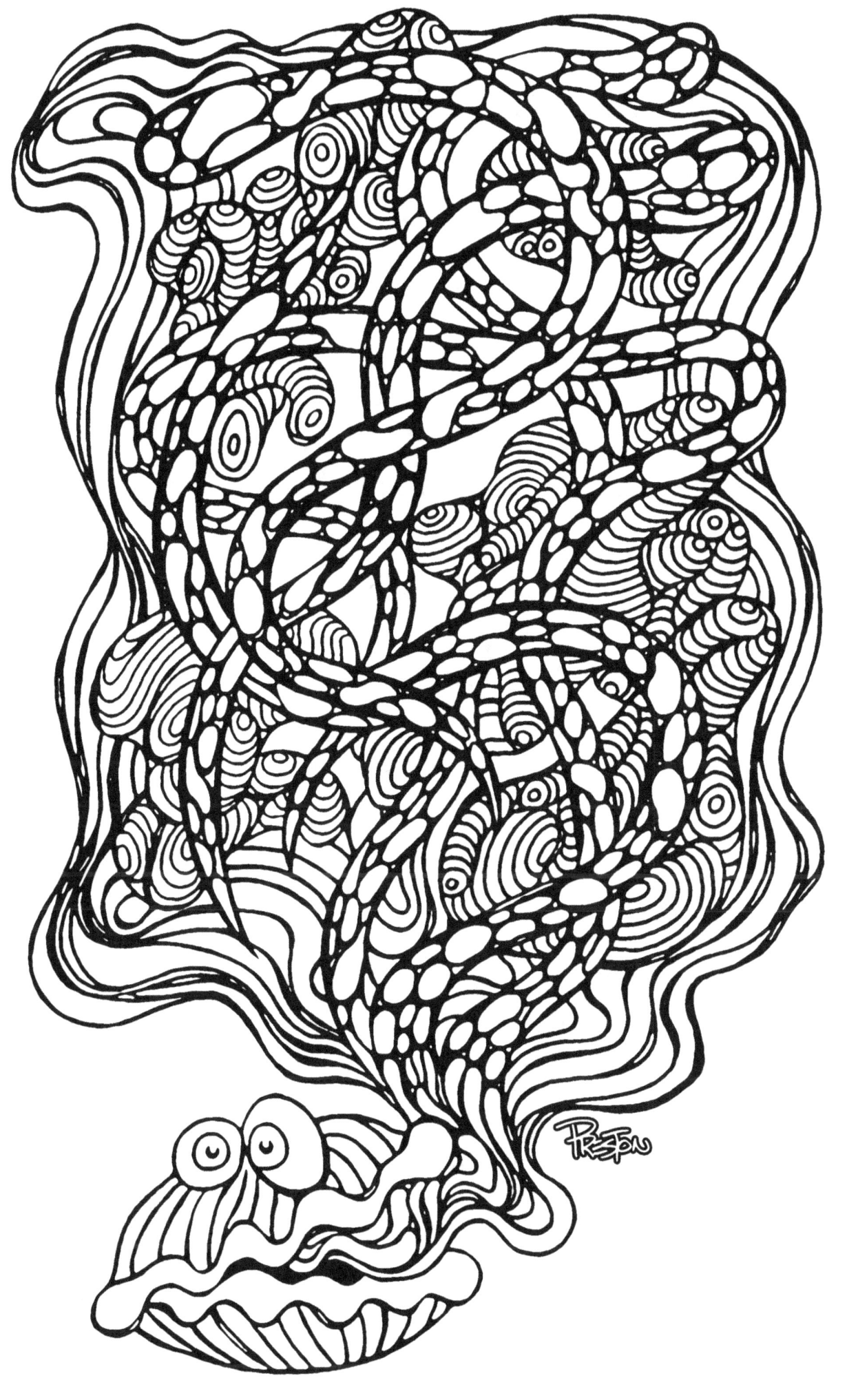

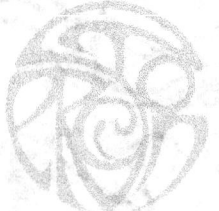

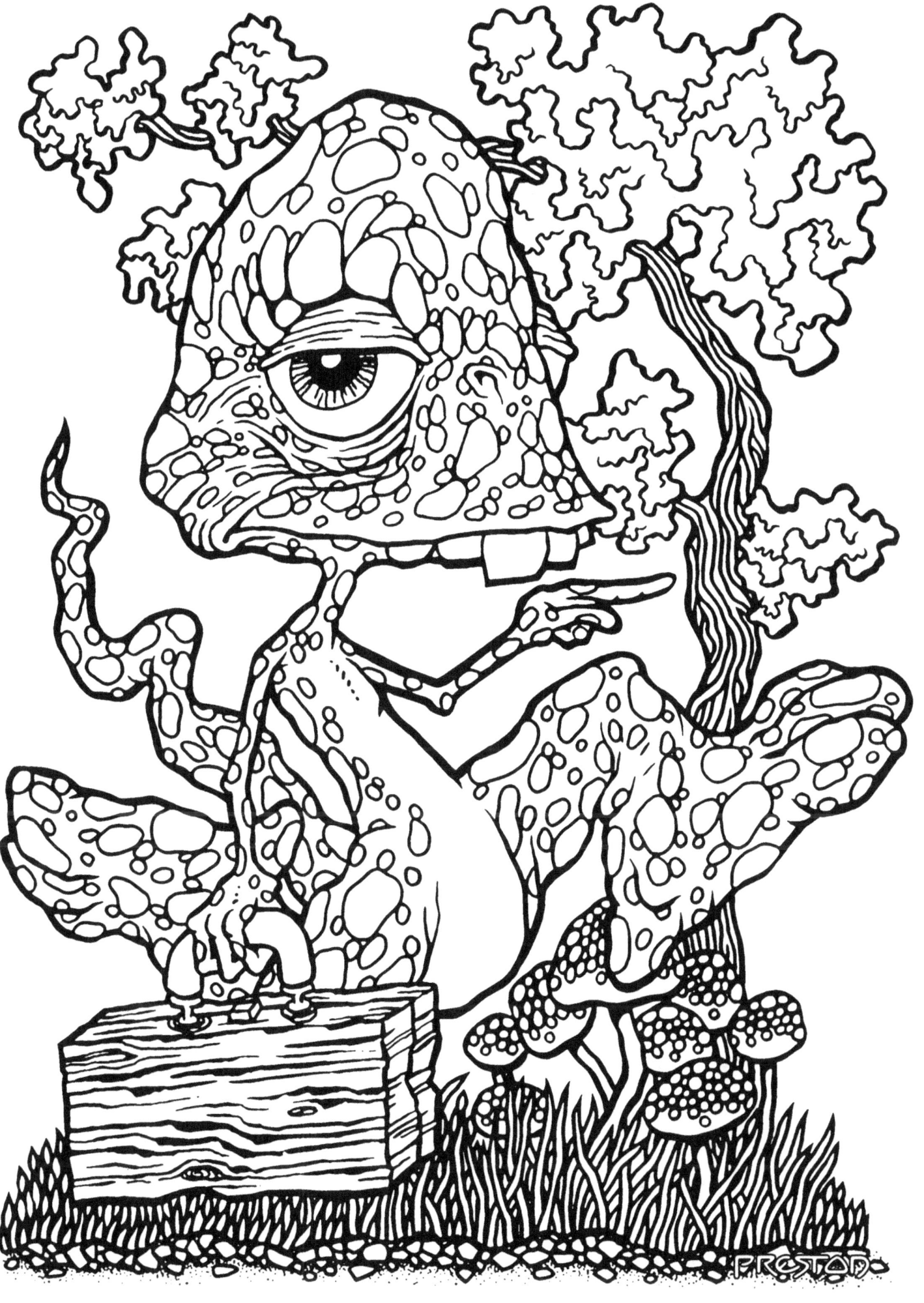

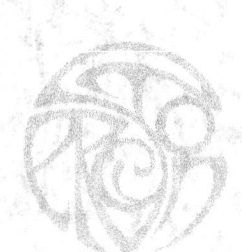

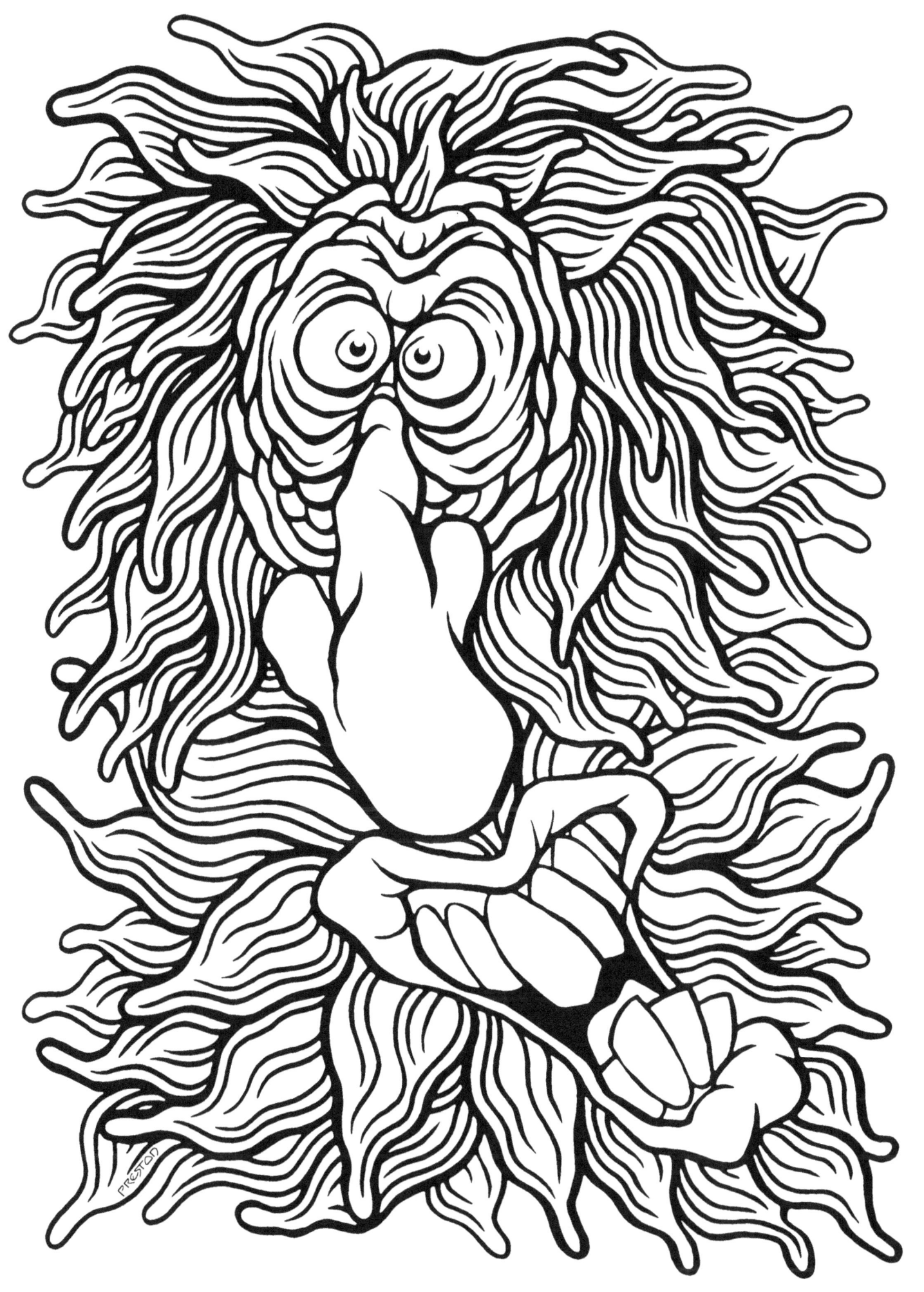

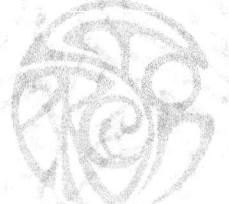

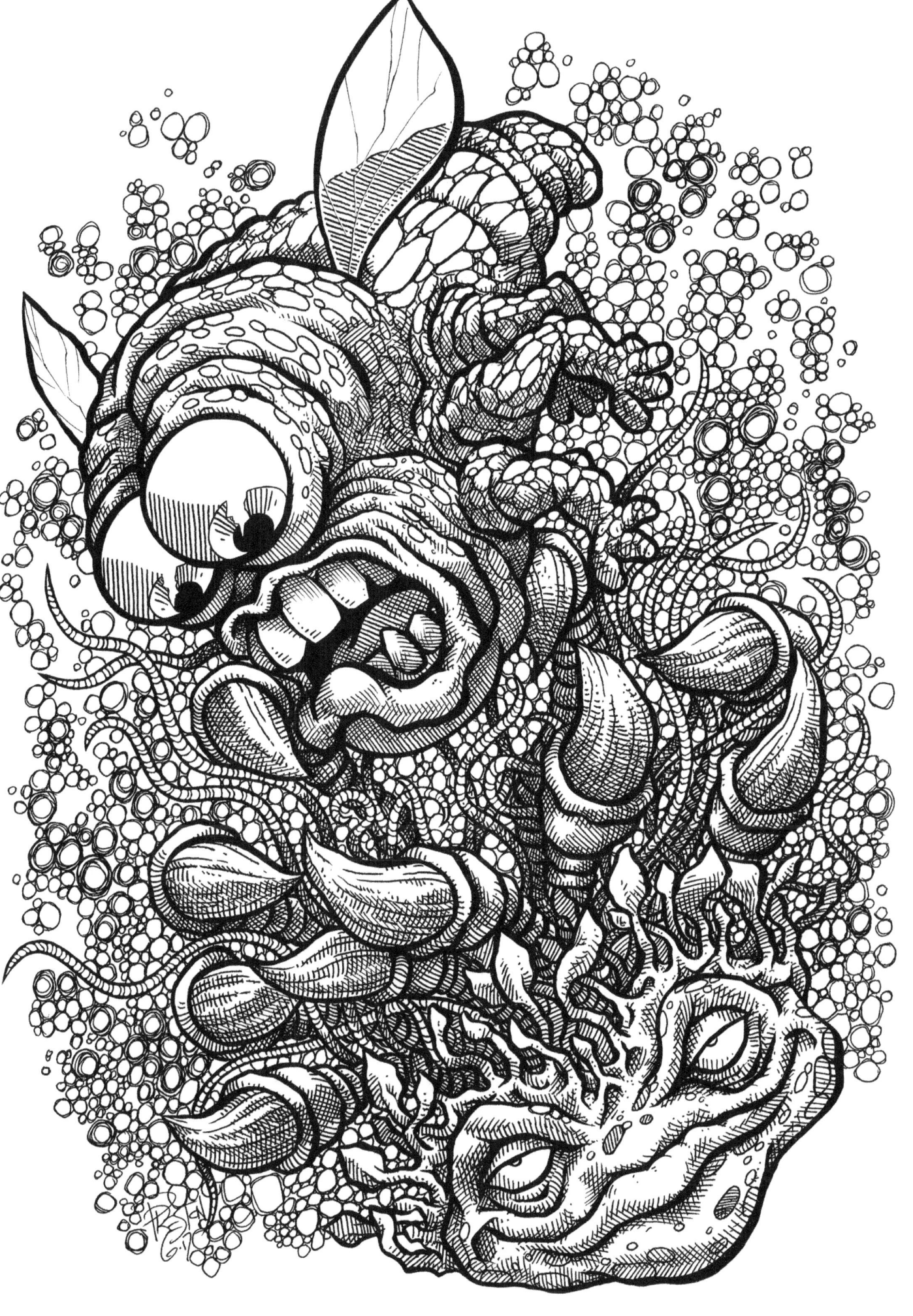

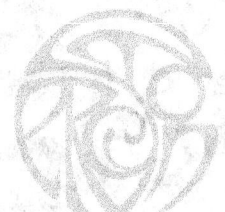

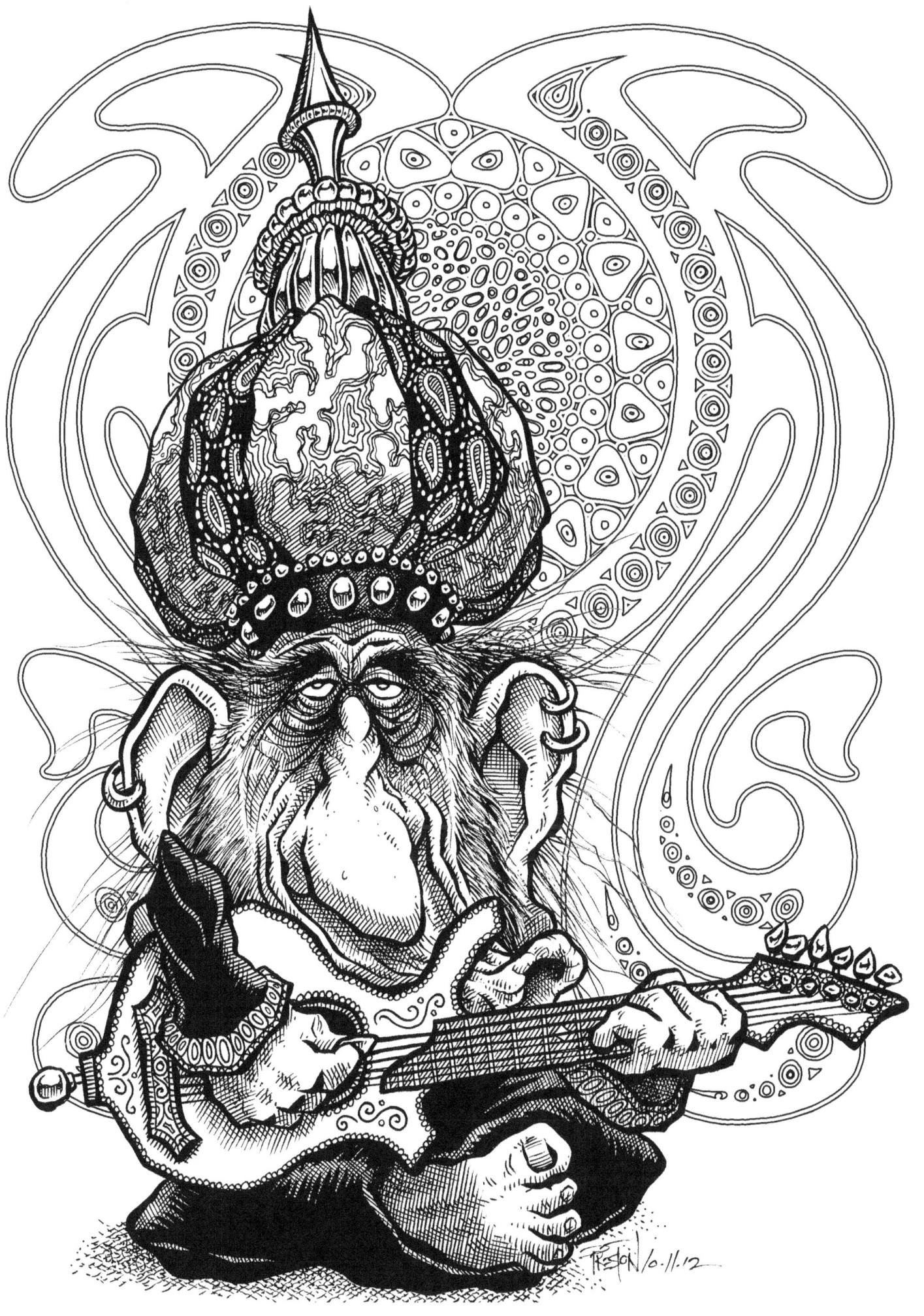

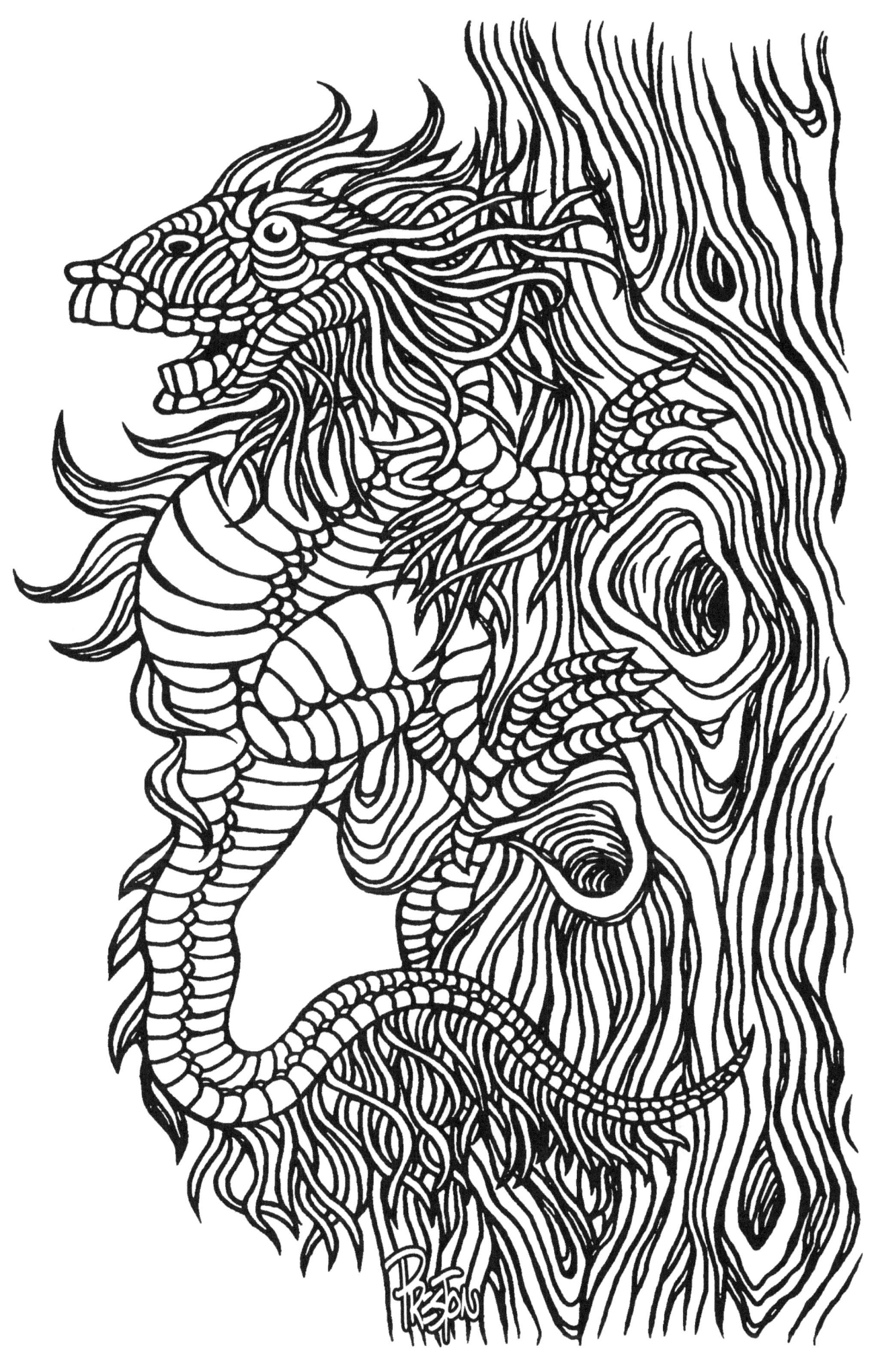

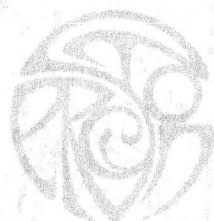

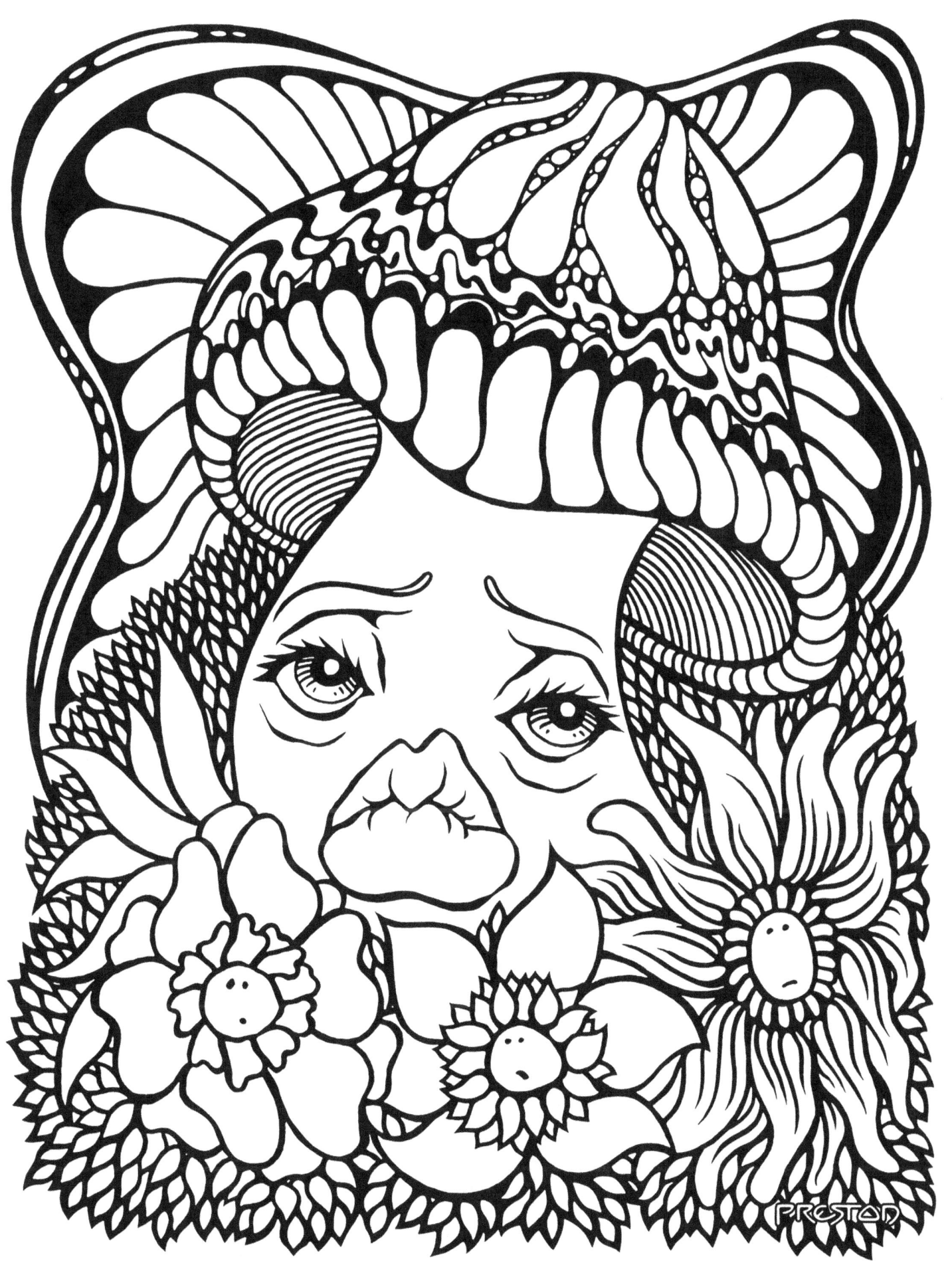

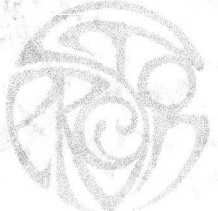

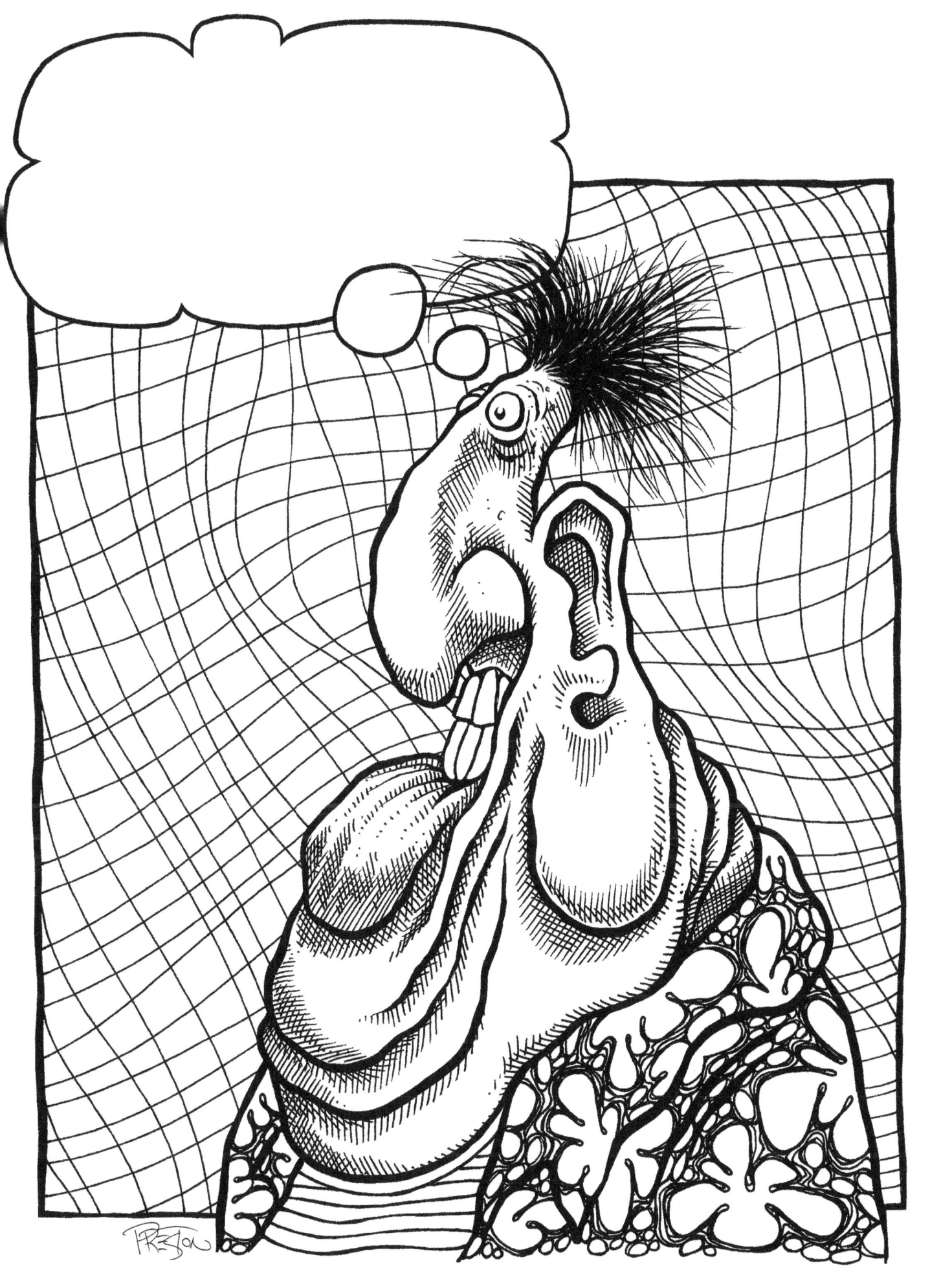

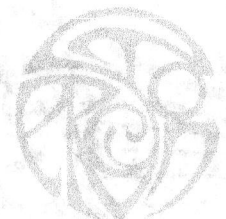

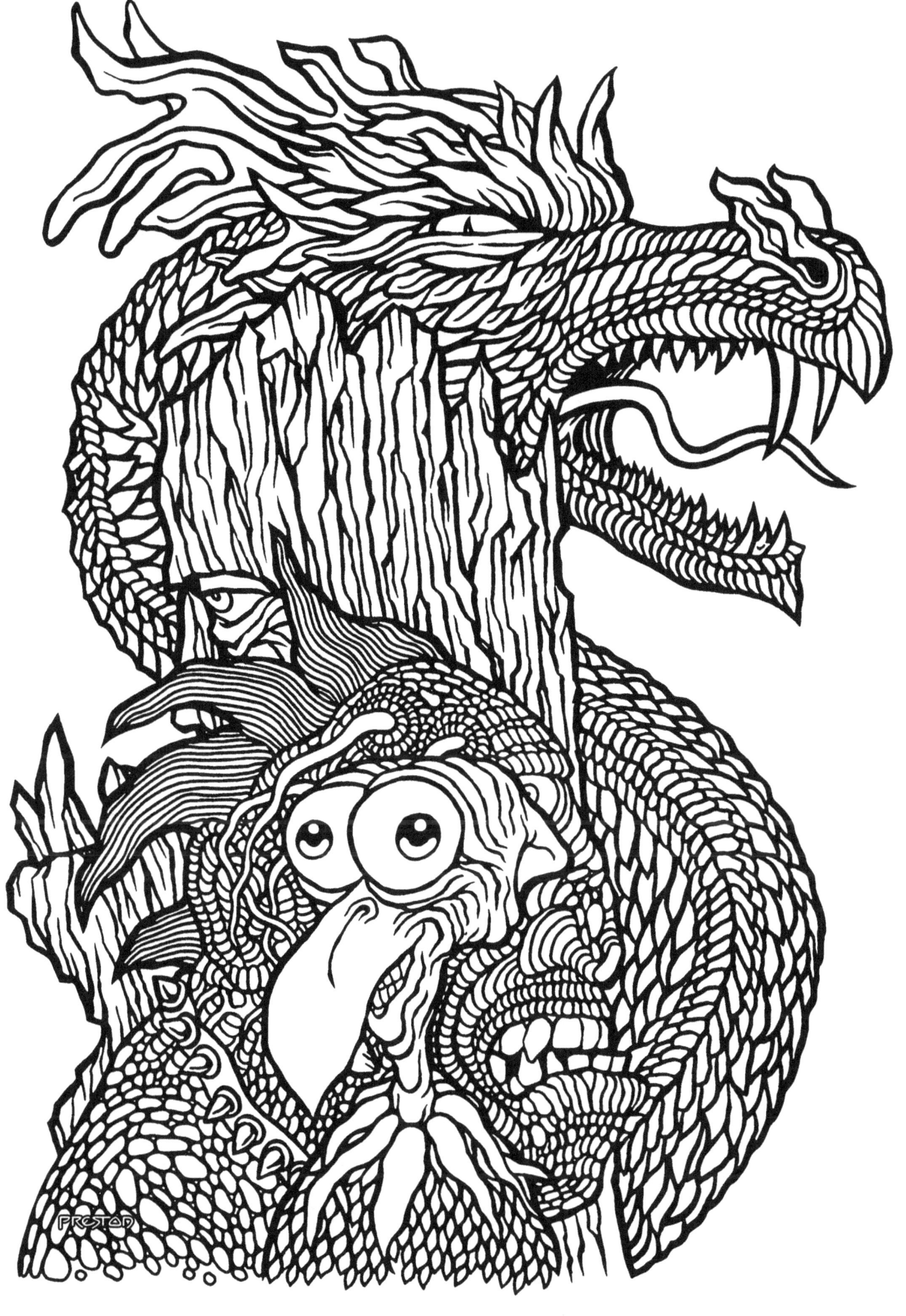

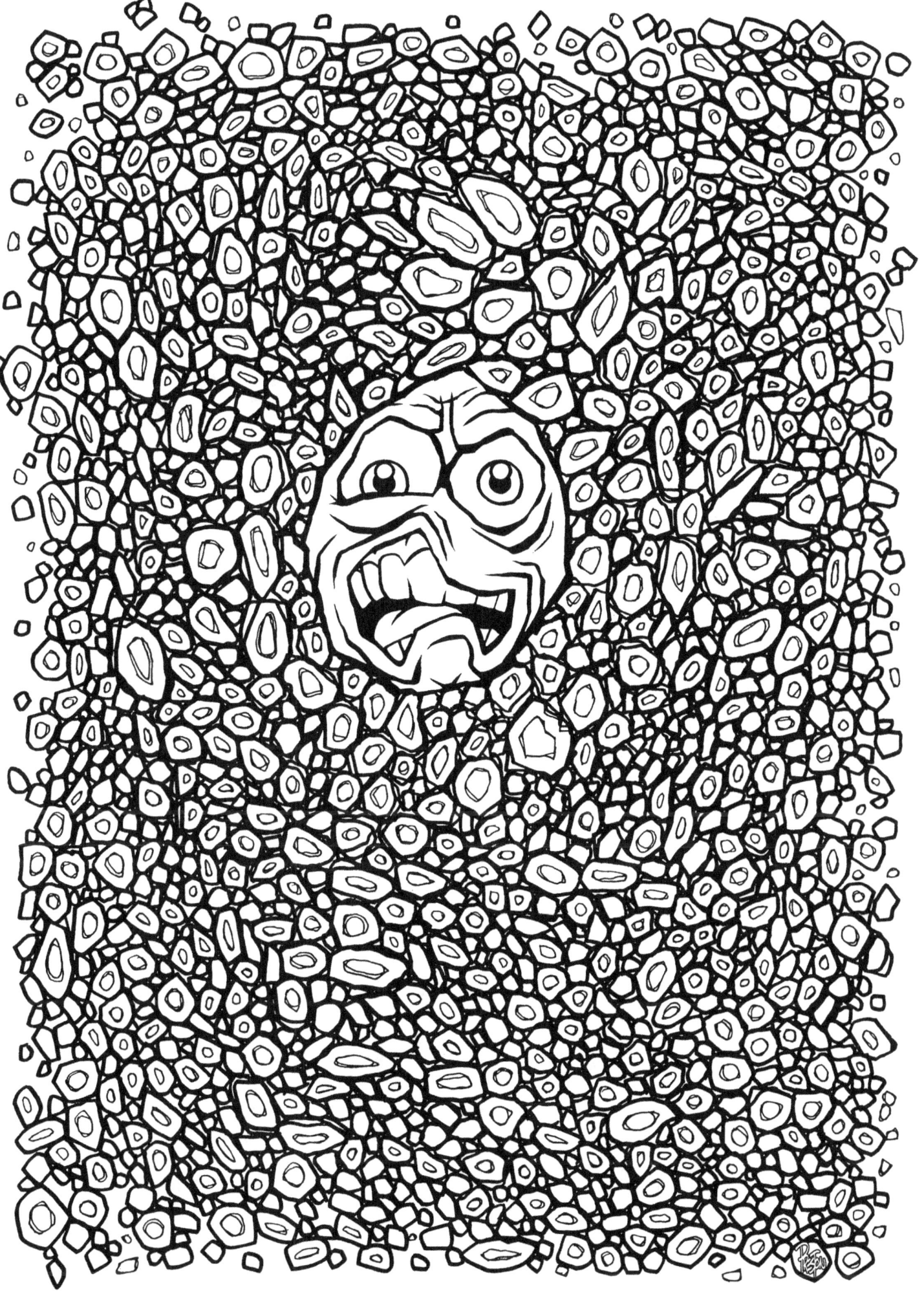

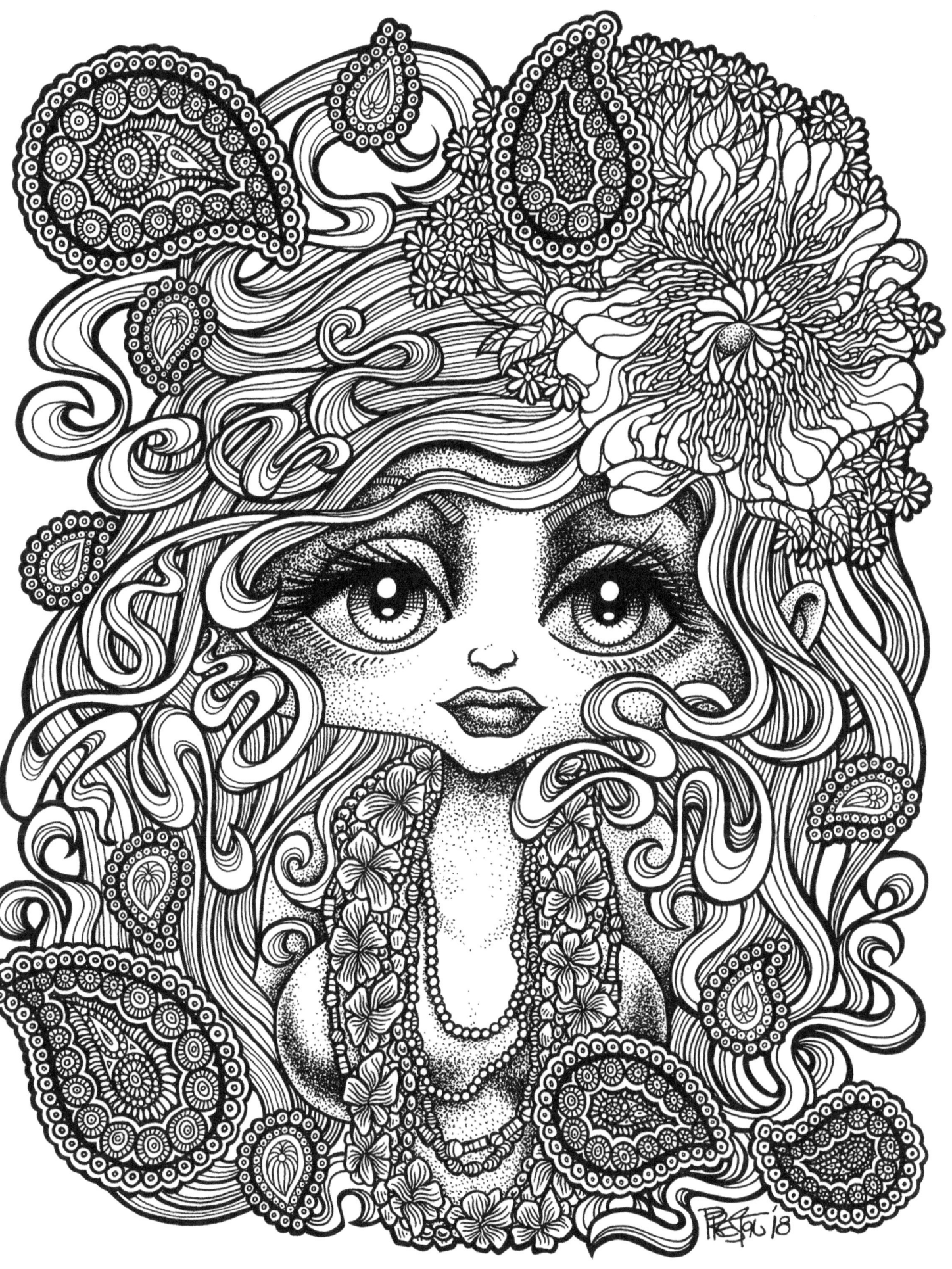

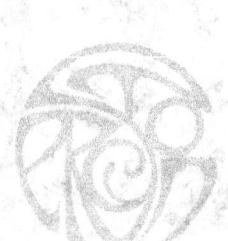

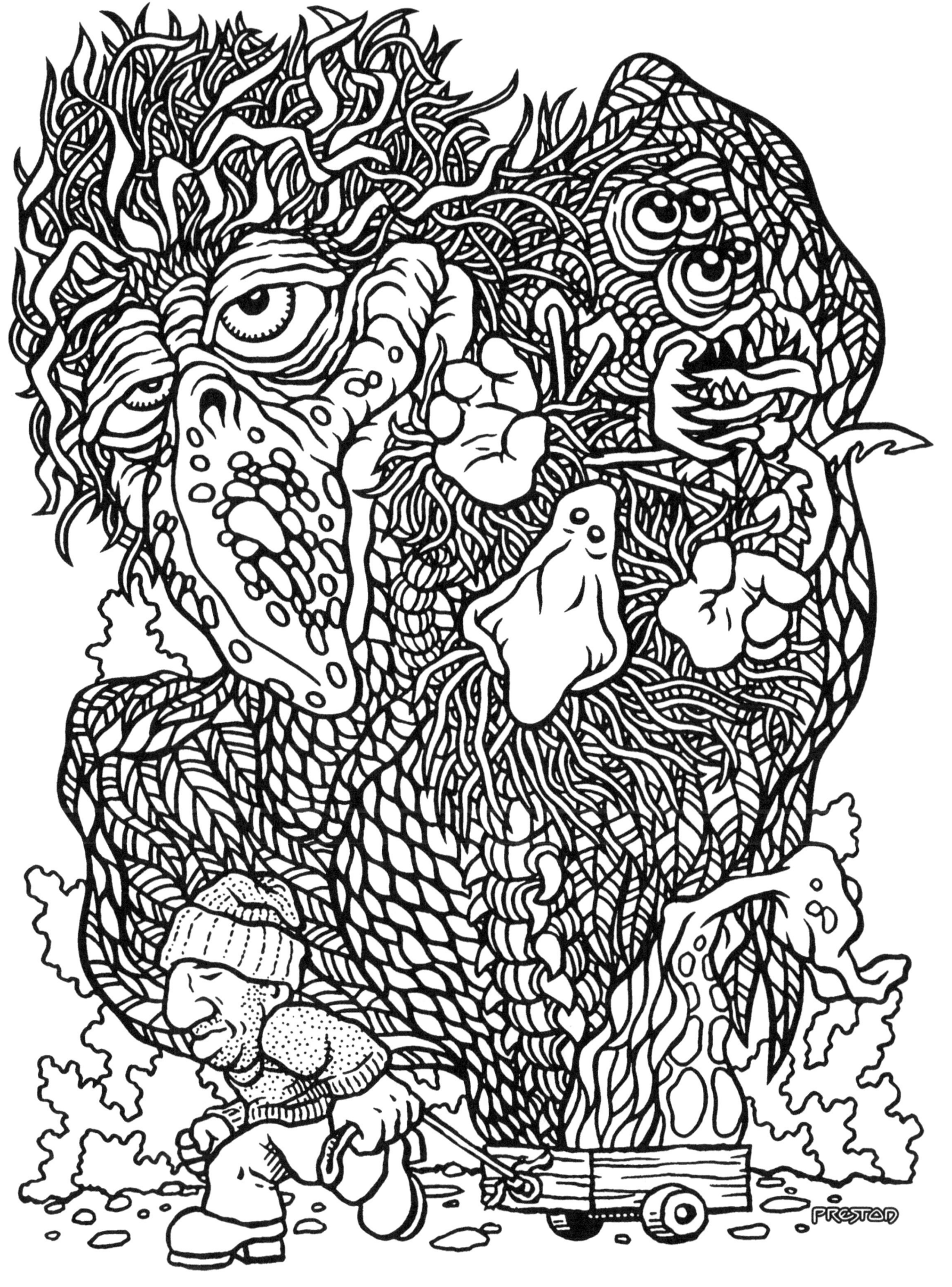

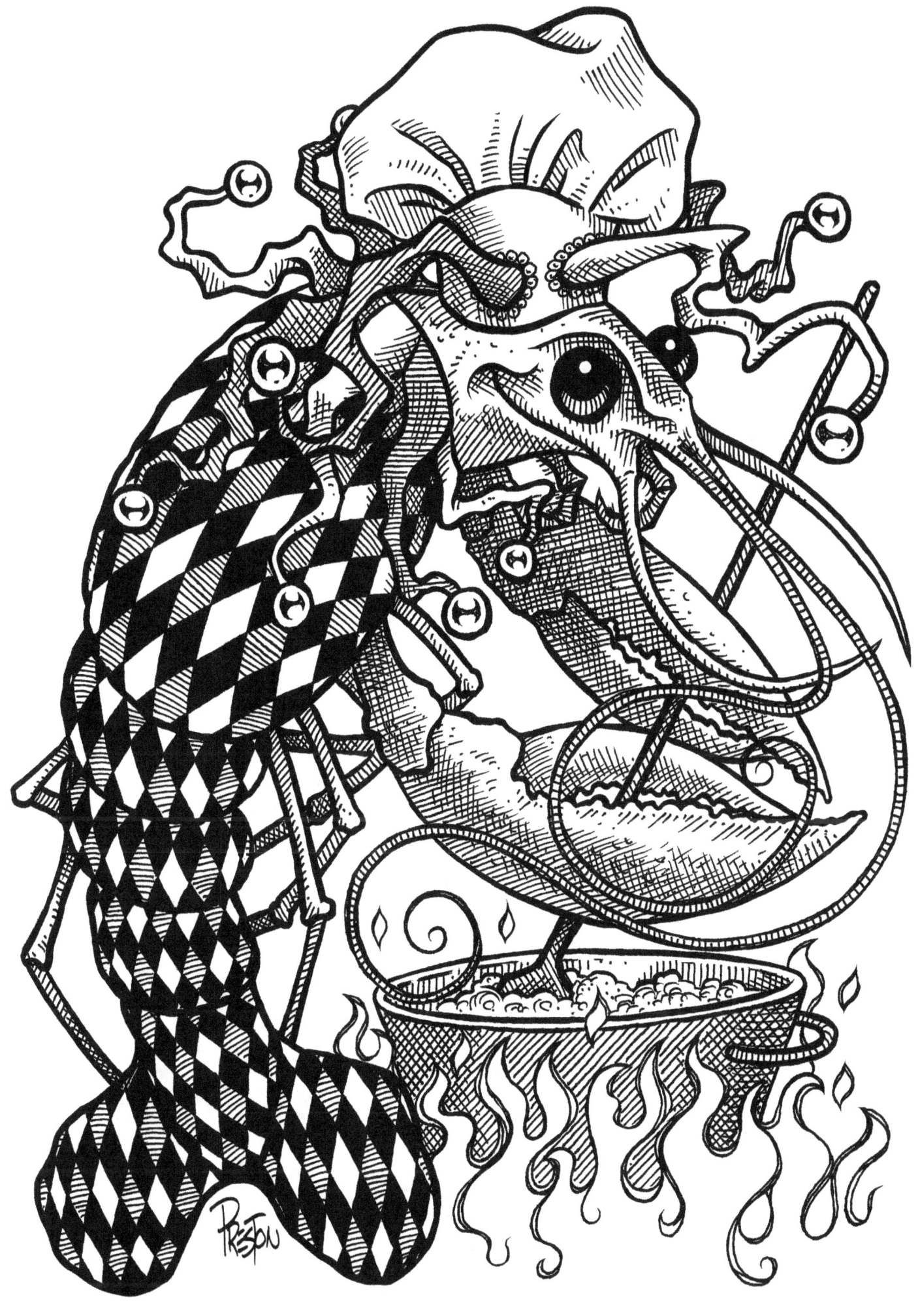

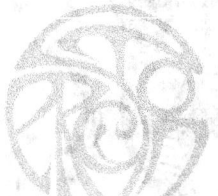

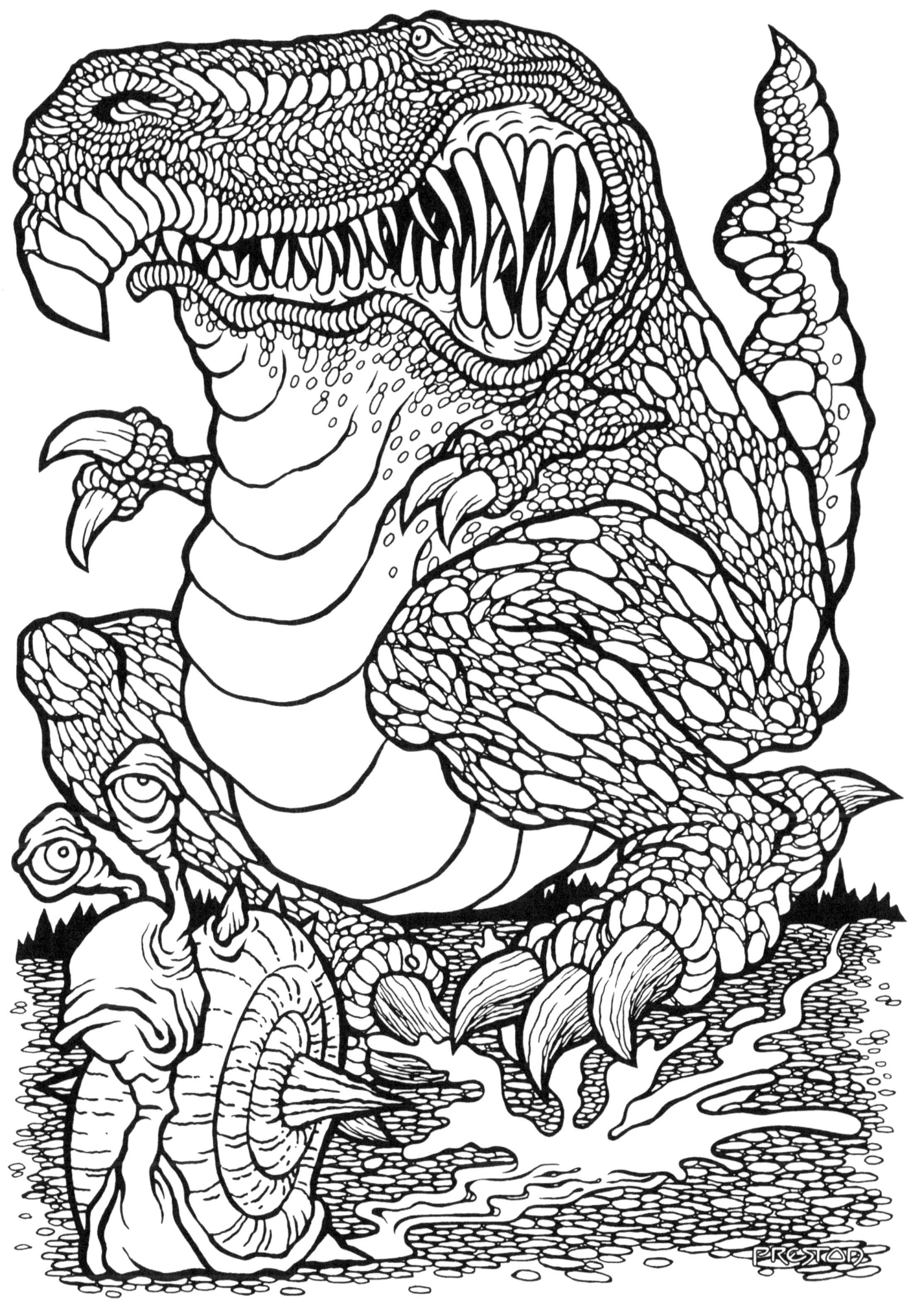

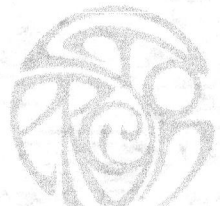

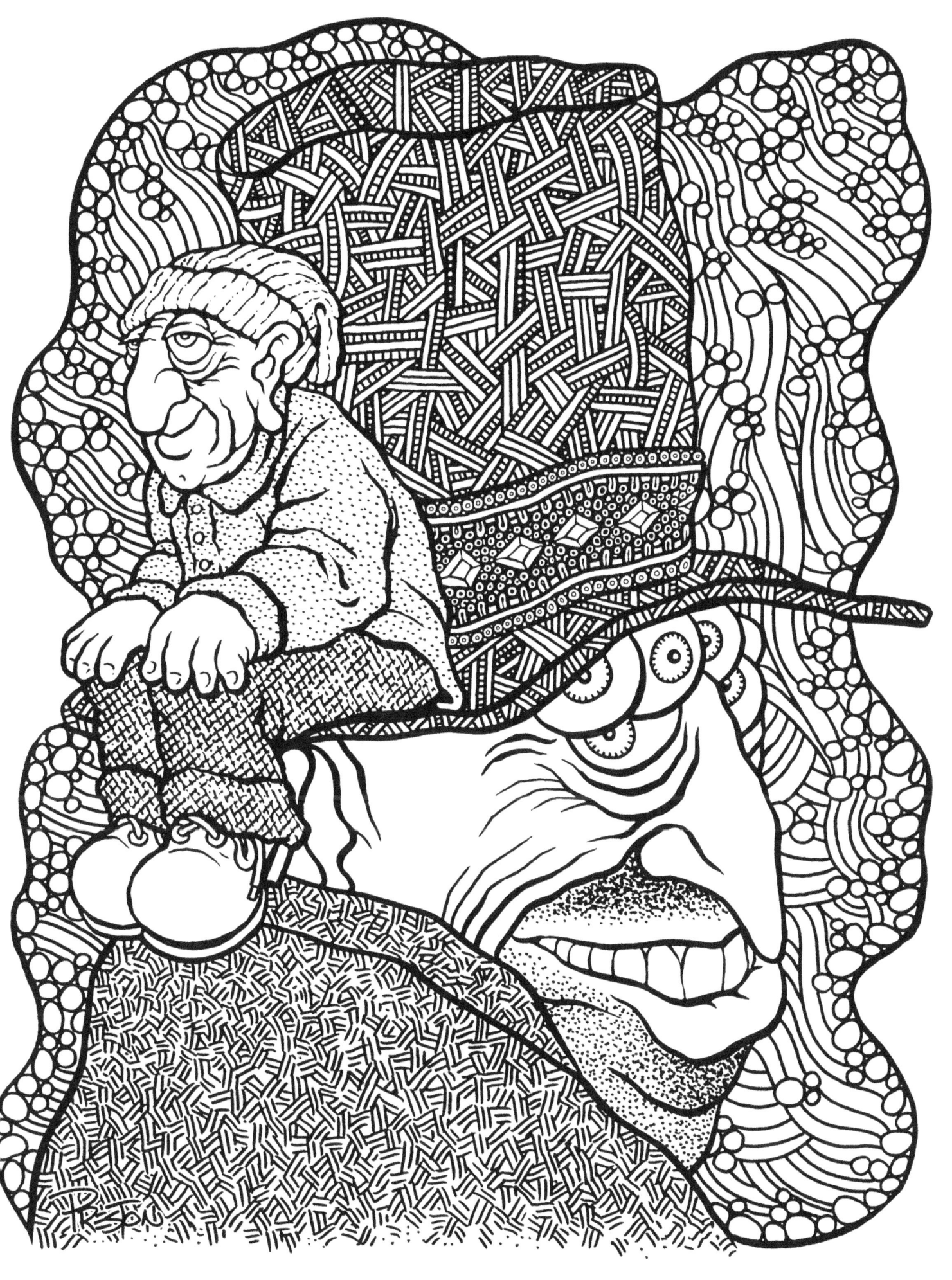

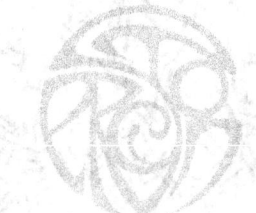

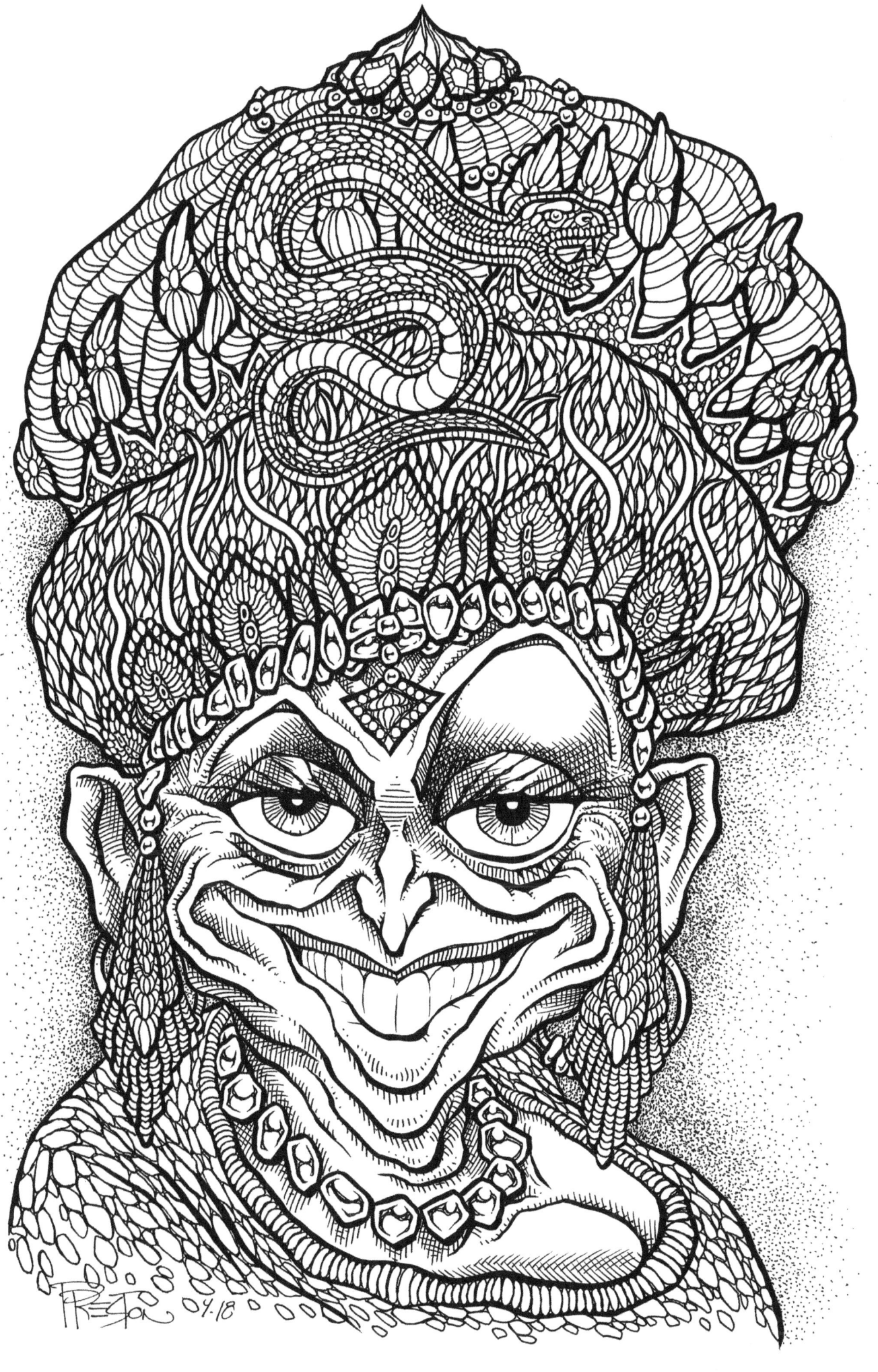

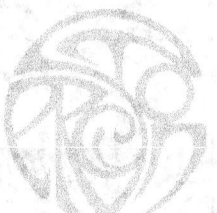

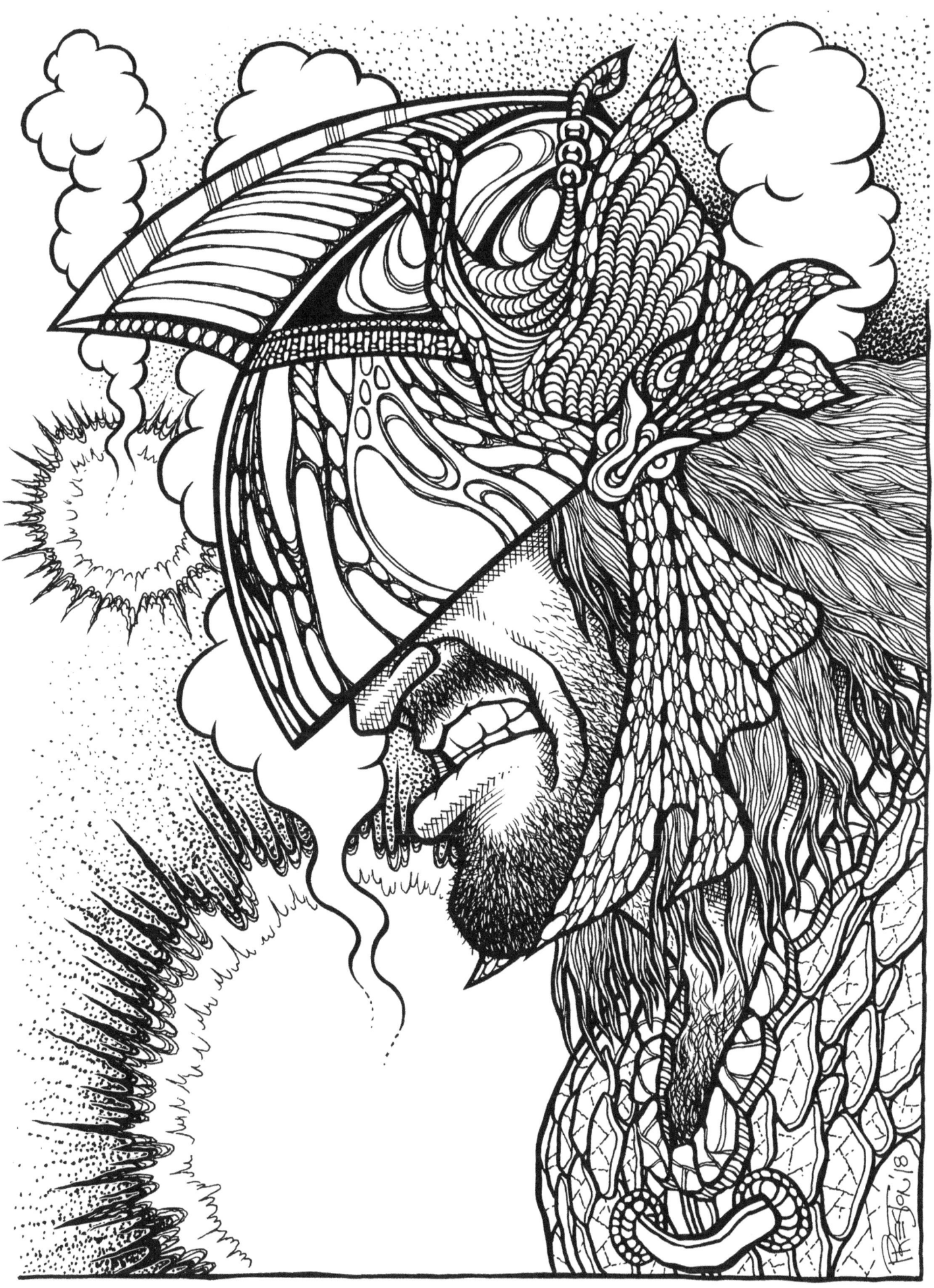

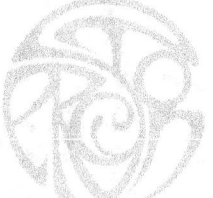

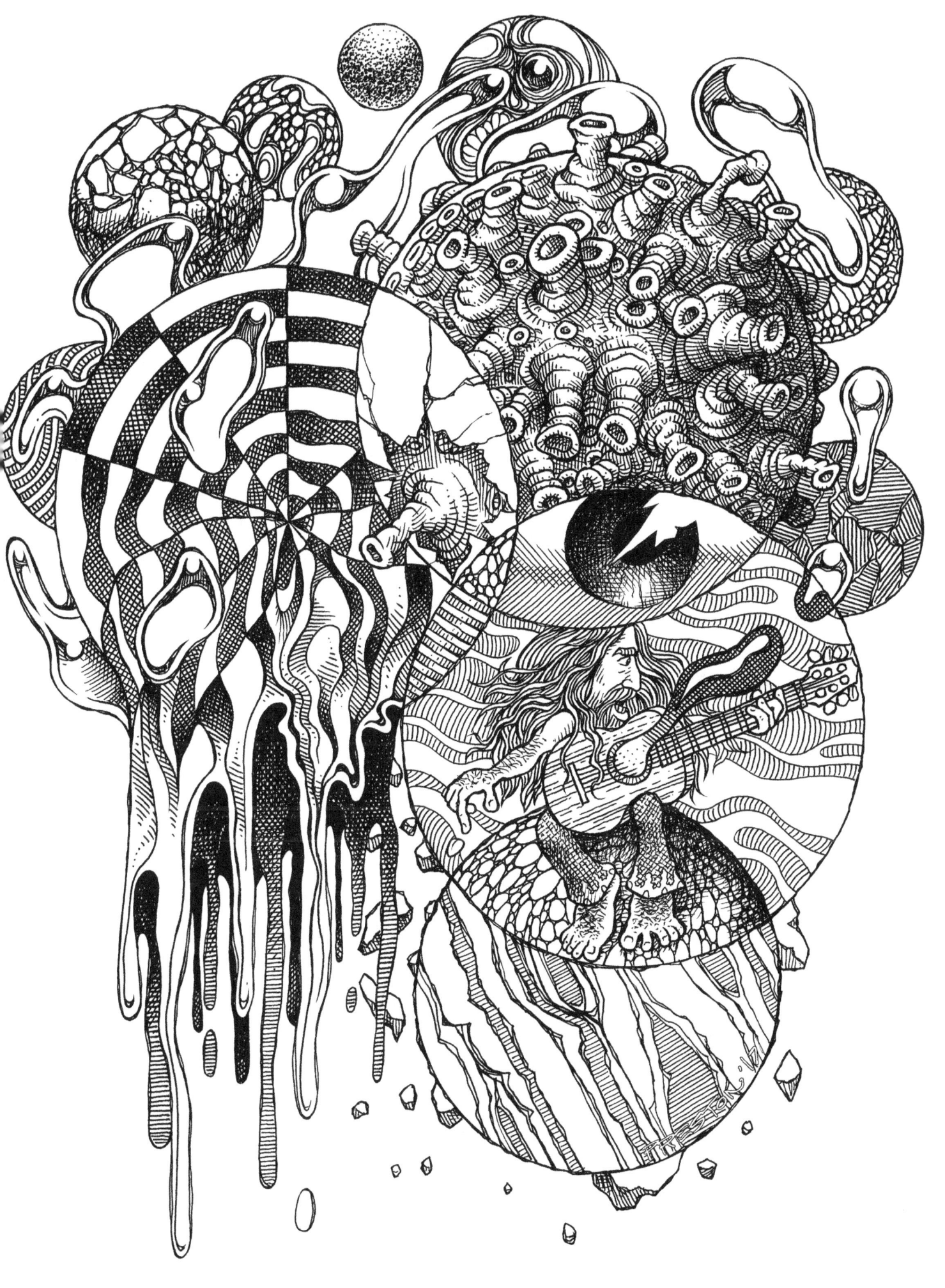

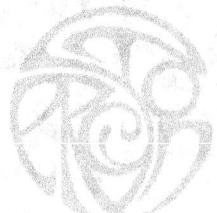

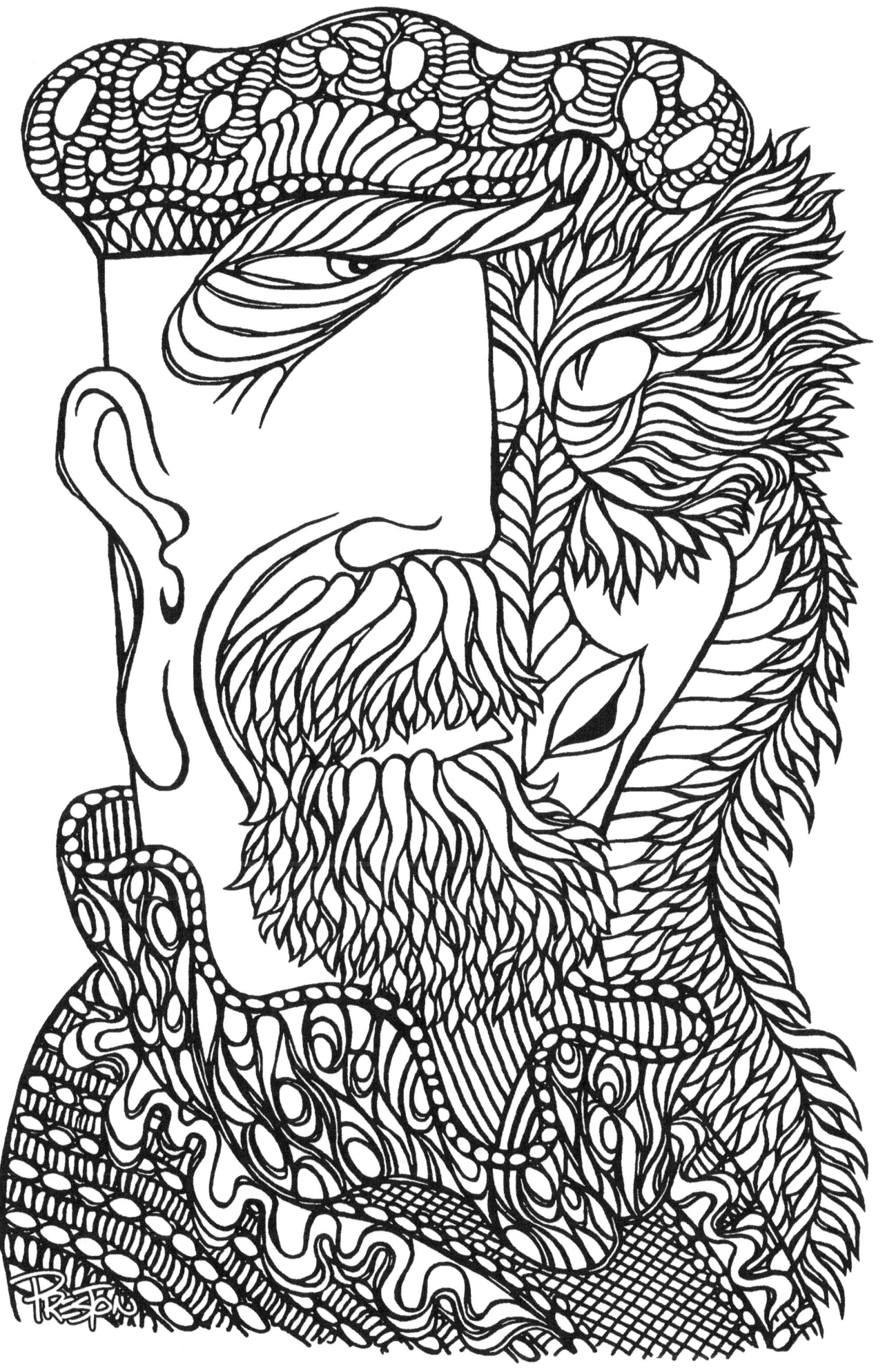

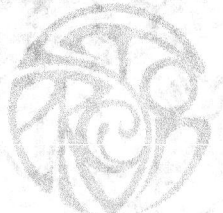

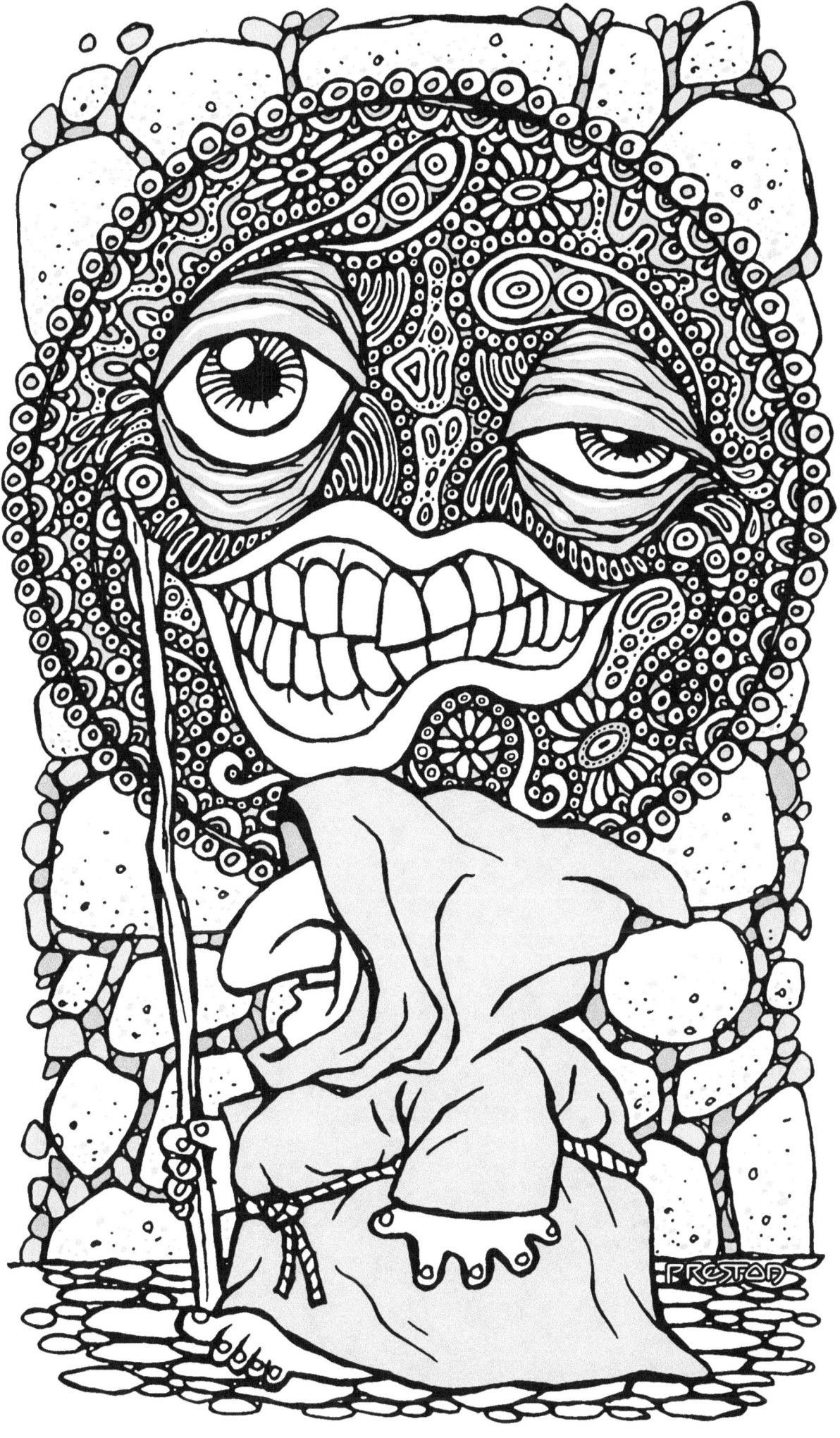

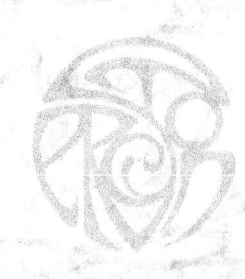

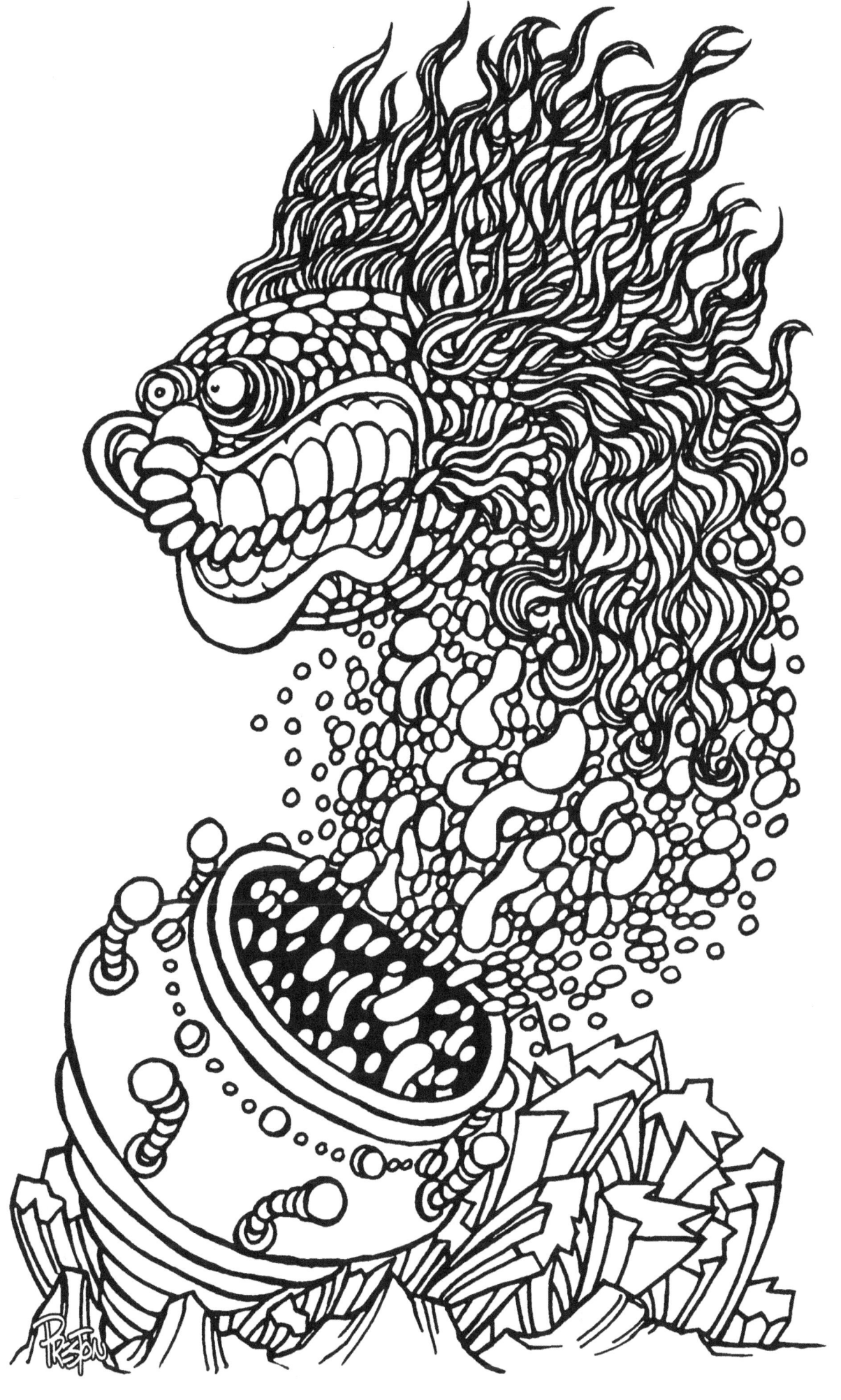

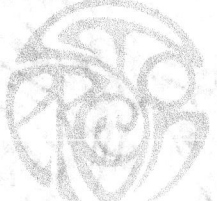

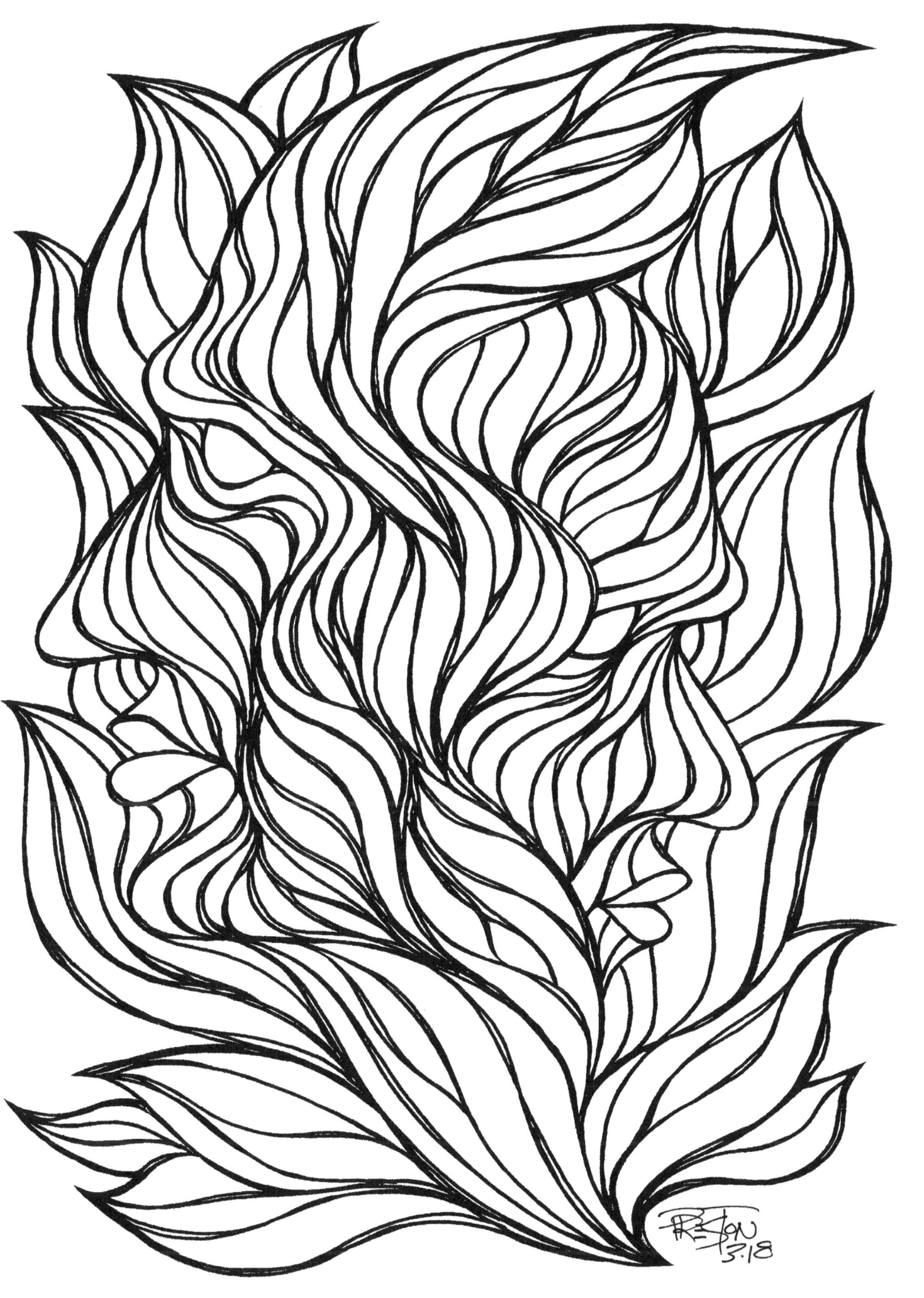

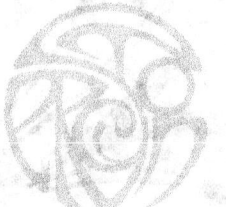

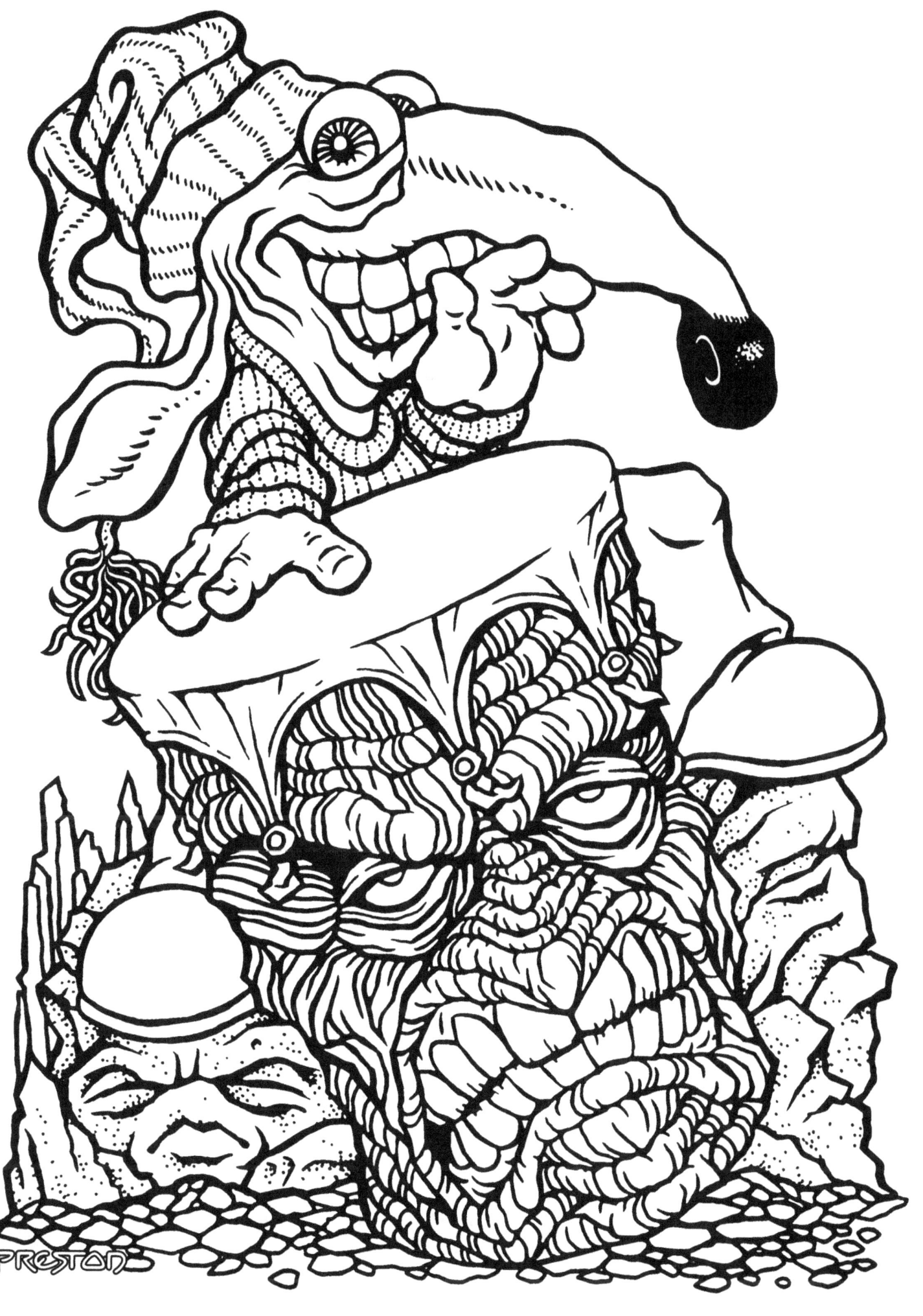

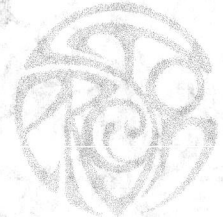

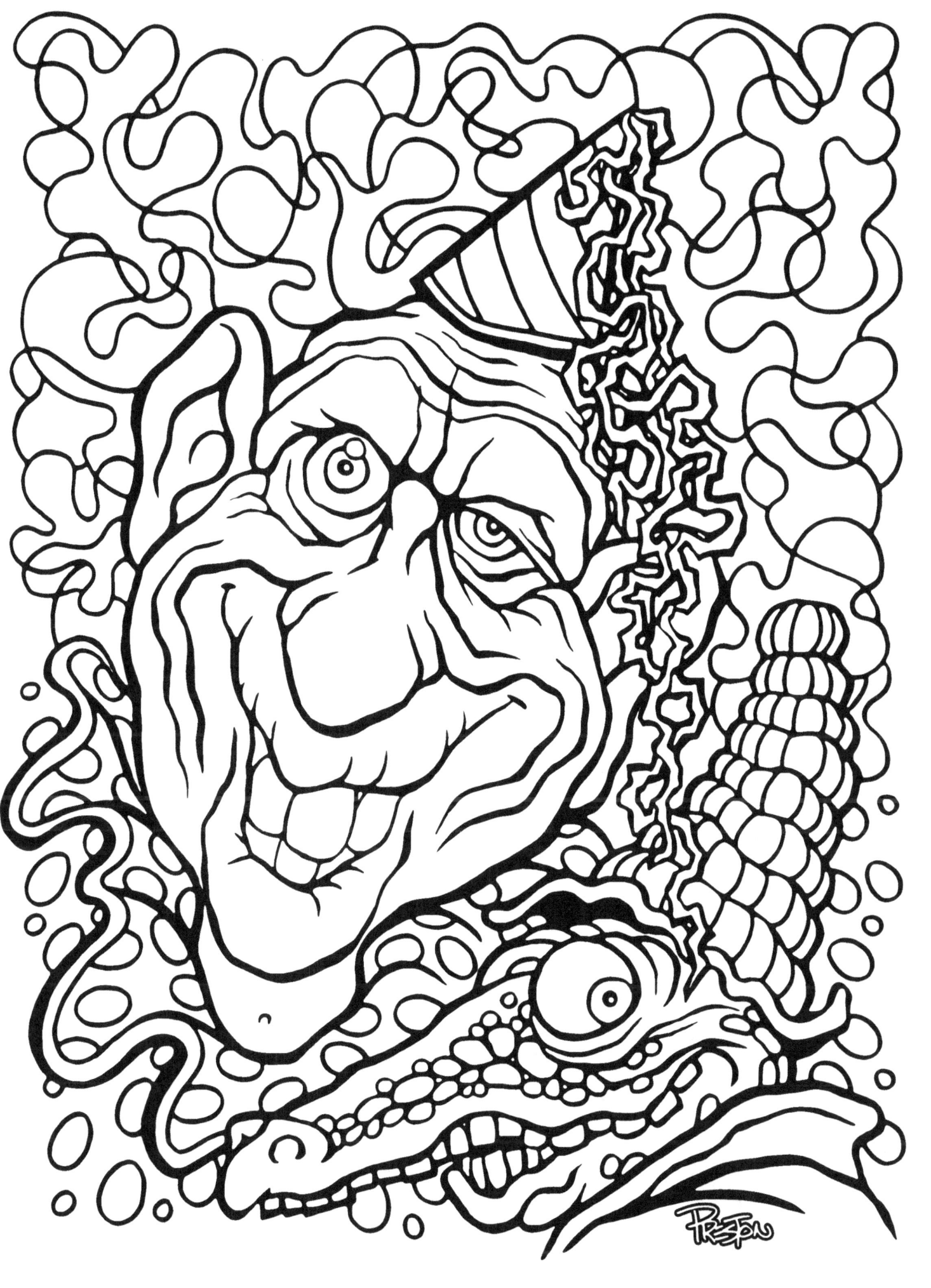

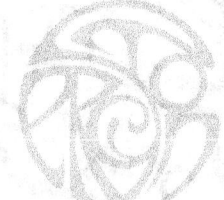

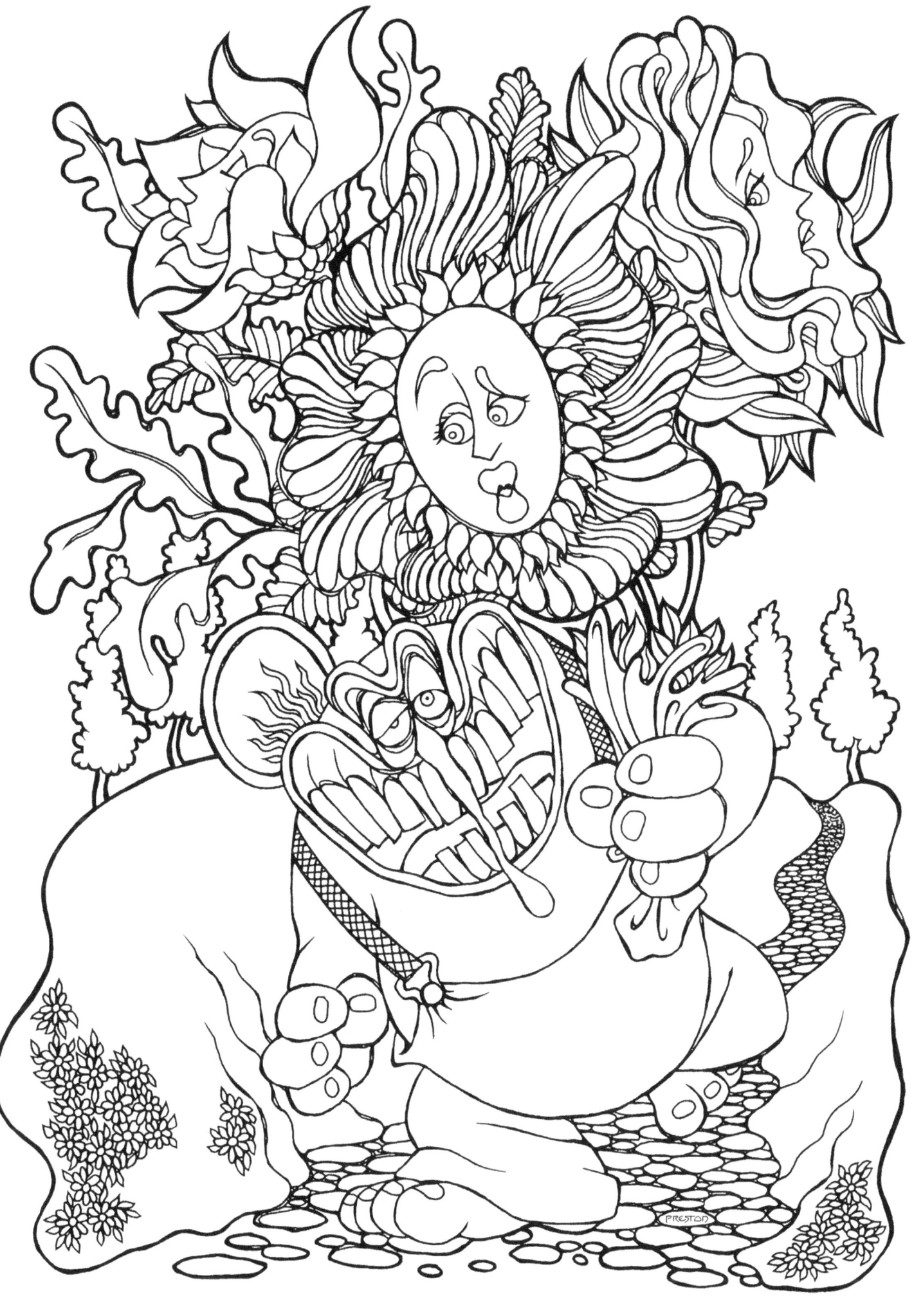

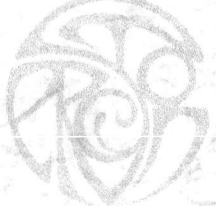

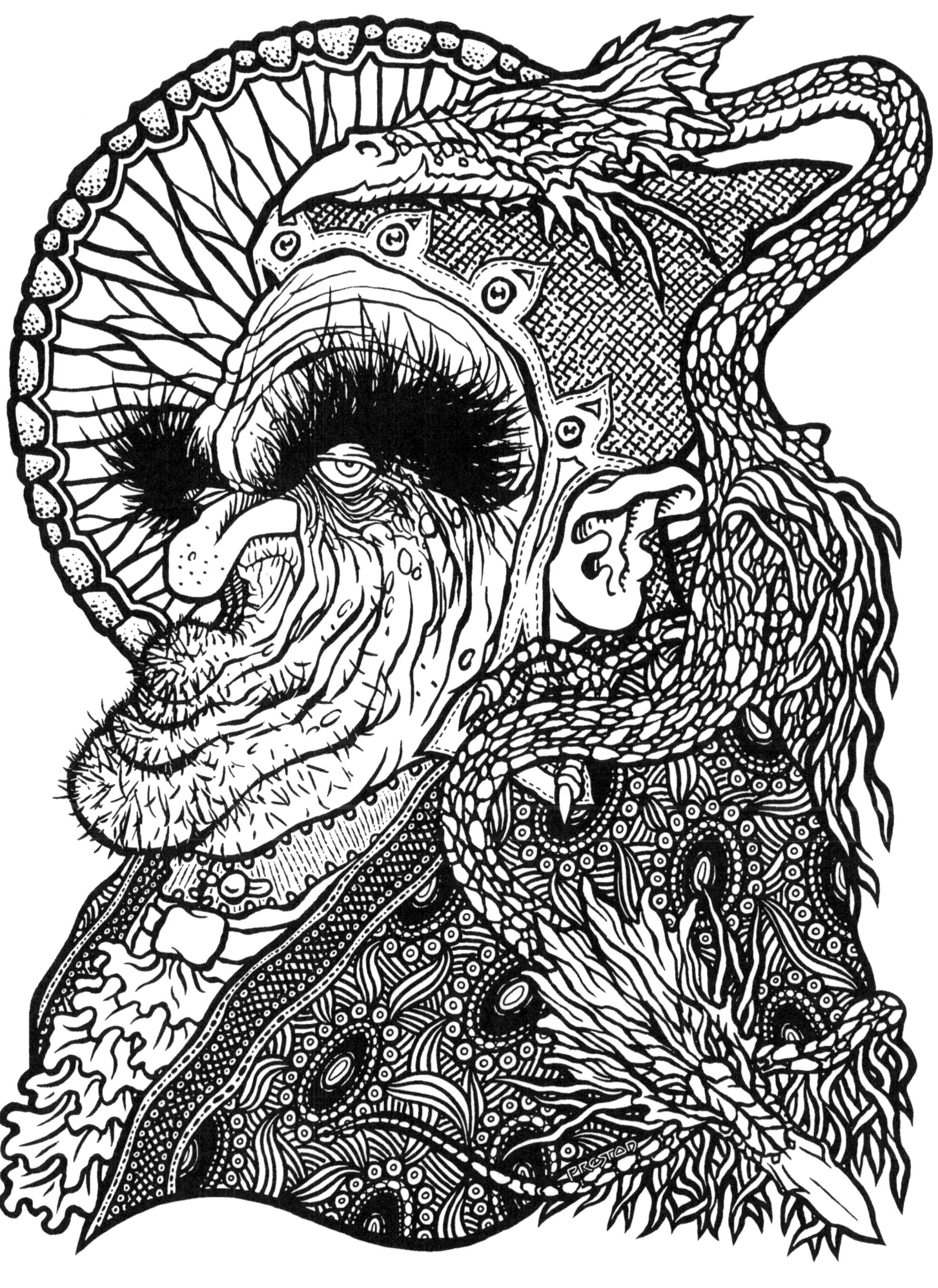

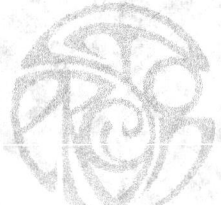

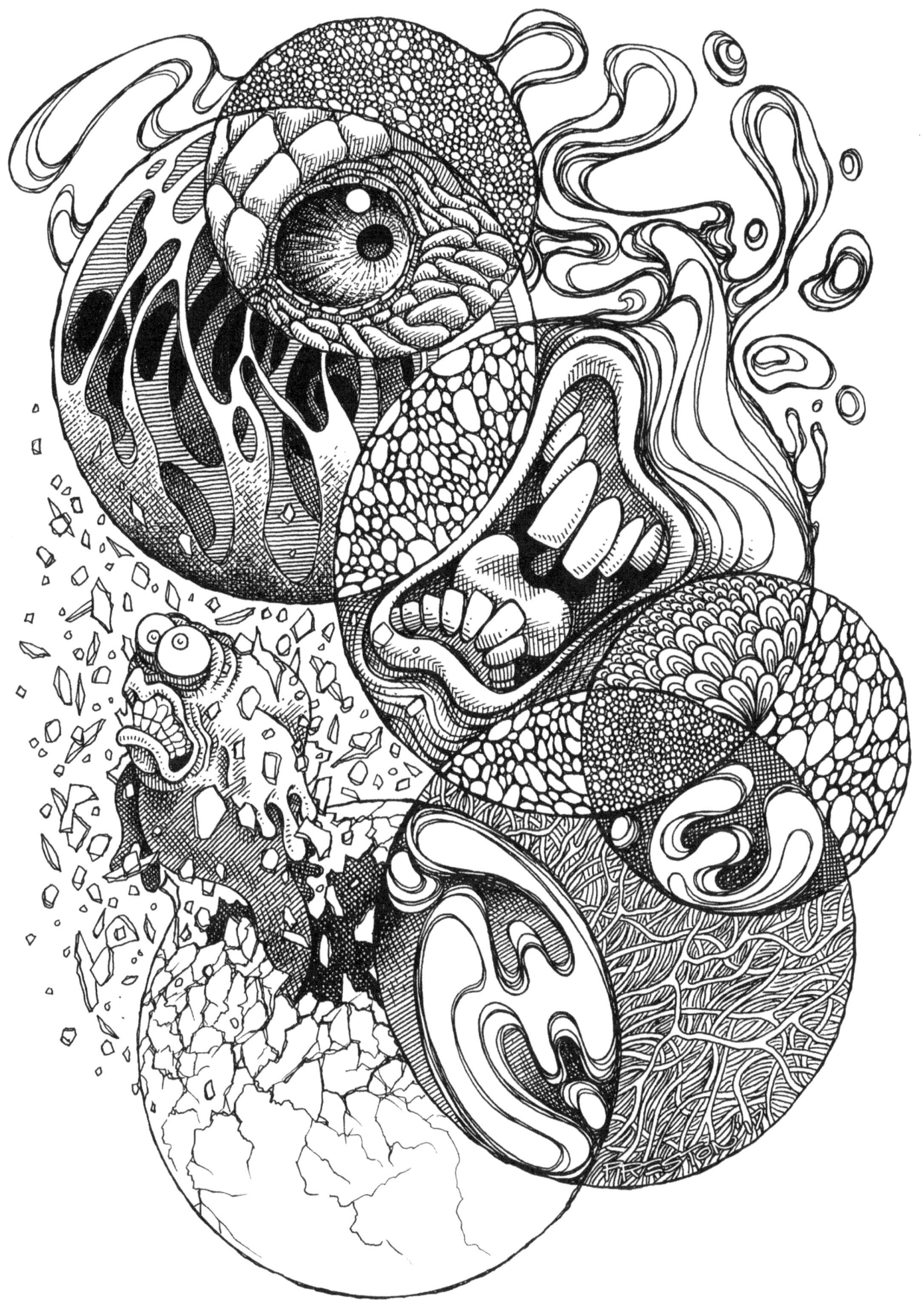

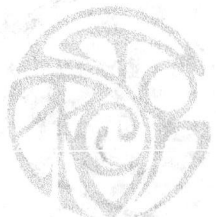

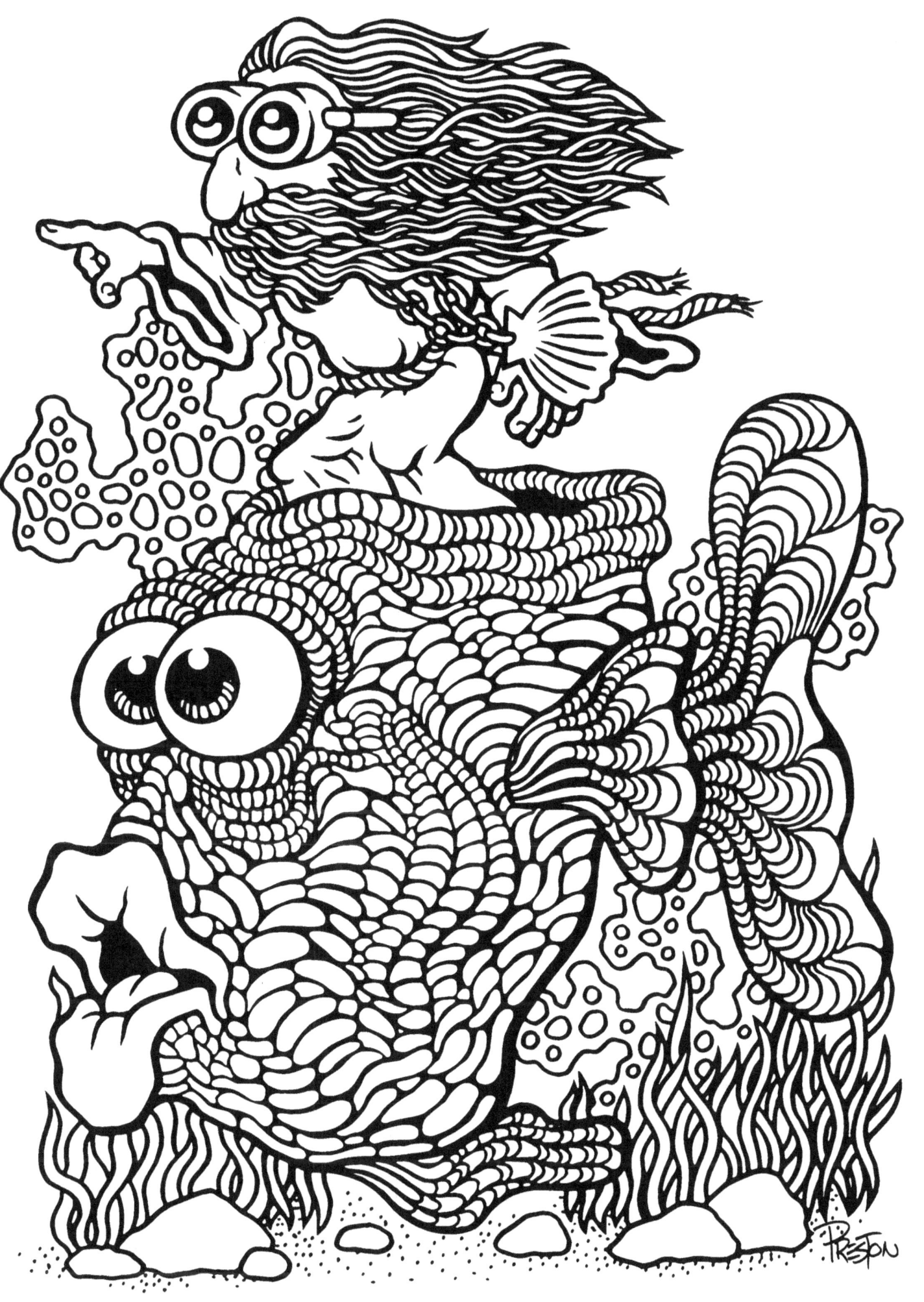

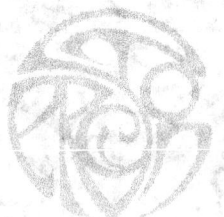

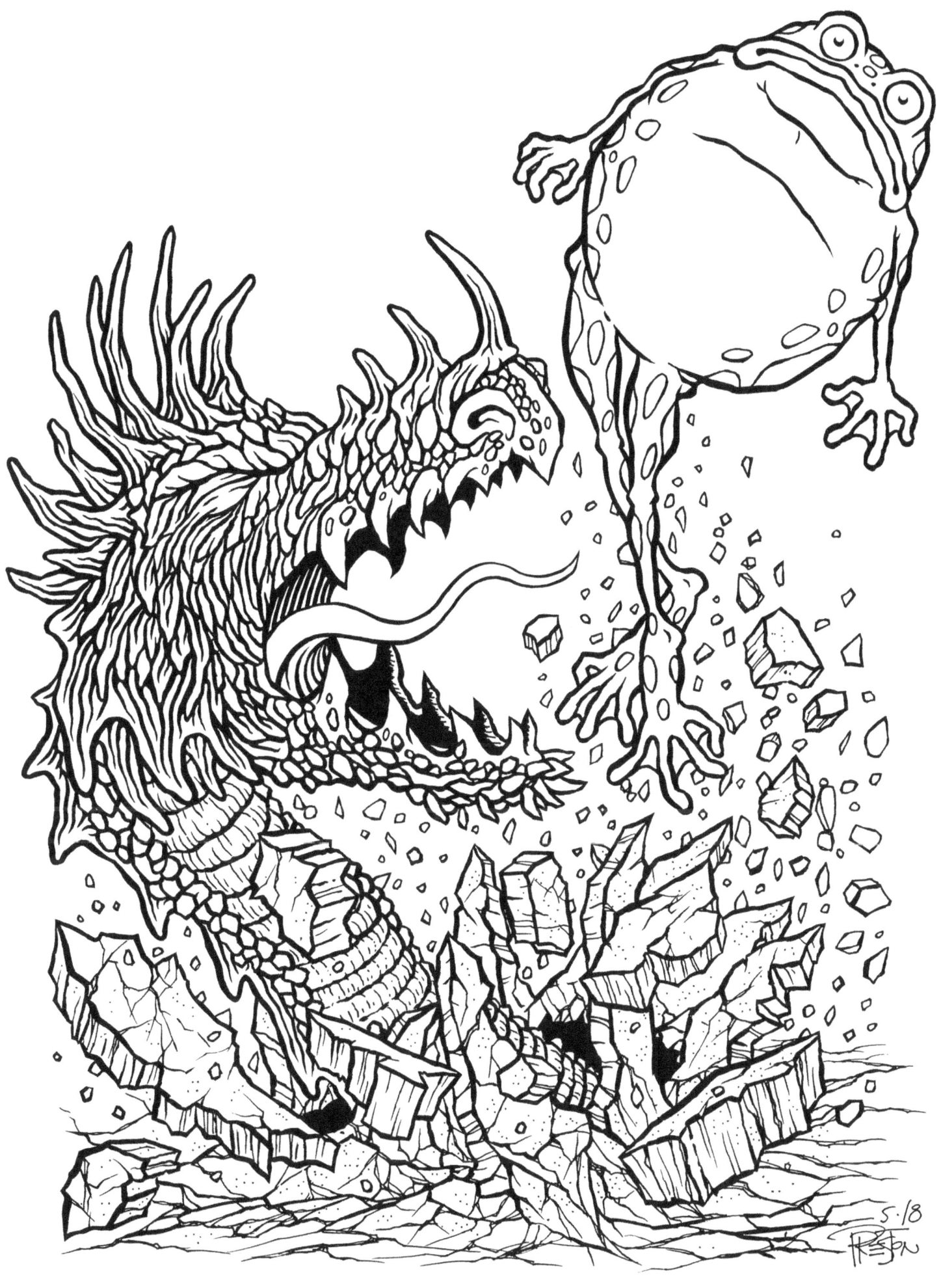

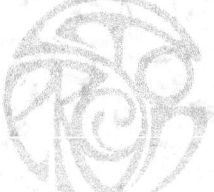

www.ingramcontent.com/pod-product-compliance
Lightning Source LLC
Chambersburg PA
CBHW081211180526
45170CB00006B/2304